THE KNOWLEDGE

Also by Victor Steffensen

Fire Country: How Indigenous fire management could help save Australia

Looking After Country with Fire: Aboriginal burning knowledge with Uncle Kuu, illustrated by Sandra Steffensen

The Trees: Learning tree knowledge with Uncle Kuu, illustrated by Sandra Steffensen

Animals on Country: Let's look after the animals with Uncle Kuu, illustrated by Sandra Steffensen

THE KNOWLEDGE

Learning from ancestral wisdom to save our challenging global environment

VICTOR STEFFENSEN

murdoch books
Sydney | London

Published in 2026 by Murdoch Books, an imprint of Allen & Unwin

Murdoch Books Australia
Cammeraygal Country
83 Alexander Street, Crows Nest NSW 2065
Phone: +61 (0)2 8425 0100
murdochbooks.com.au
info@murdochbooks.com.au

Murdoch Books UK
Ormond House, 26–27 Boswell Street,
London WC1N 3JZ
Phone: +44 (0) 20 8785 5995
murdochbooks.co.uk
info@murdochbooks.co.uk

NATIONAL LIBRARY OF AUSTRALIA

A catalogue record for this book is available from the National Library of Australia

A catalogue record for this book is available from the British Library

ISBN 978 1 76150 086 2

Cover design by Laura Thomas
Map on back cover: American Geographical Society Library, University of Wisconsin-Milwaukee Libraries
Cover background image: Cause/Affect
Author photograph on page 274 by Tazmyn Slicer
Typeset by Midland Typesetters, Australia
Printed and bound in Australia by the Opus Group

Murdoch Books acknowledges the Traditional Owners of the Country on which we live and work. We pay our respects to all Aboriginal and Torres Strait Islander Elders, past and present.

EU Authorised Representative: Easy Access System Europe, Mustamäe tee 50, 10621 Tallinn, Estonia, gpsr.requests@easproject.com

10 9 8 7 6 5 4 3 2 1

Dedicated to all who can act and see.

Aboriginal and Torres Strait Islander readers are advised that this book may contain names of people who have died.

Murdoch Books will donate $1 from the sale of each copy of this book to the Living Knowledge Network.

CONTENTS

GLOSSARY OF TERMS

Note: In this book, except where otherwise stated, 'Indigenous' and 'Aboriginal' refer to Indigenous and Aboriginal peoples in the country we now call Australia.

Ancestors Ancestral beings who belong to the land and everything on it and the seas and everything in them, and who followed the traditional Indigenous laws; people from whom a group or an individual is descended.

back-burn Process to burn an area of land, often to control a wildfire or in advance of the fire season; usually burning into or against the wind.

biochar Charcoal produced by burning the vegetation; can fertilise the soil and store carbon dioxide.

burn zone Designated area to be burned.

bush Australian name for forest; a natural landscape and ecosystem; land covered with vegetation.

bush regeneration Process of bringing areas of land back to their natural state, by replacing exotic plants and native weeds with species native to that landscape.

camp burn Cultural burn around houses and towns to protect them in the event of a wildfire, or to protect traditional dwellings in the times of the Old People.

clear-fell To cut down and remove or push into a pile every tree in an area.

contract burn Fire practitioners contracted by a government agency, business or organisation to carry out a burn.

cool burn/cool fire Traditional practice in which the cool temperature of the burn means soil is not scorched; the smoke from the burn is white instead of the dark, heavy smoke of a wildfire. A cool burn can reduce the risk of wildfire and encourage renewed plant growth.

coolamon A curved wooden vessel, usually carved by Indigenous men; Indigenous women used it to carry water, foods and seeds, for example, and as a cradle for babies.

corroboree Ceremony of singing, dancing and storytelling, often involving the whole Indigenous community in an area or many communities in a region.

Country An English word used by Aboriginal people to acknowledge the environment and all geographical features of nature. It is also a term used to recognise each other as having a relational connection with Mother Nature.

cultural burning Cultural burning ensures the fire is kept cool, so it does not bake the soil, which destroys the organic matter; the tree canopies are not scorched, so their flowering season is not affected. Cultural burning practices have evolved to benefit Country and Mother Nature.

cuz A relative of the same generation who is not a brother or sister; a friend.

Dreaming A realm referred to by Aboriginal people as the time of creation and how people have culturally evolved from that time, which is still acknowledged through story, dance, song and traditional practices today.

drip torch Hand-held fuel canister with a spout and wick from which the fire is ignited when it touches the ground; used when back-burning to set fire to vegetation.

dugong Aquatic mammal found in warm waters off the coast of Australia and other countries. Dugongs feed on seagrass meadows.

ecosystem An ecosystem (ecological system) includes all living things in an area; it is the way these living things interact with each other and with the soil, climate and other non-living aspects of the environment; ecosystems may be known by the dominant species growing in an area, such as a eucalypt ecosystem.

Elder Indigenous person held in high regard and has a position of authority in their community; Indigenous knowledge holders.

firebreak Strip of land that has been cleared to stop the spread of fire; a natural firebreak might be a waterway that the fire can't jump.

fire zone Area where a wildfire is burning or may be about to burn.

fire-dependent Country/ecosystem Ecosystem that relies on regular cool burning of the vegetation to renew the lifecycle for that Country.

fire-sensitive Country/ecosystem Ecosystem that can be sensitive to fire. For example, some beach trees and plants growing along coastal areas in Australia are sensitive to fire and if the trees do get burned, it takes them a long time to recover.

fuel loads Build up of vegetation, including dry, dead vegetation, that will burn hot and quickly.

Gold Rush The discovery of gold and sometimes other minerals would bring a rush of miners to the area. In the nineteenth century the Gold Rush in Victoria and elsewhere in Australia and in California in the United States brought thousands of people to mine for gold in the hope of making their fortune.

gum tree Common name in Australia for any shrub or tree of the genus *Eucalyptus*, the eucalyptus tree.

harvesting Removing saplings (young trees) from around and between the parent trees to allow room for the parent trees to grow tall, wide and spread their branches to create a canopy. It is a form of

Indigenous stewardship that can help plants grow stronger and keeps their ecosystems healthy and plentiful, if done in the right way.

hazard reduction burns Fires lit and managed by rural fire services and other agencies to reduce the severity of wildfires that might occur in the future.

invasive native plants Native plants that grow in areas where they were previously not dominant. As they flourish, they can change the composition of the ecosystem that is native to that Country and eventually take over the landscape. In Australia, two examples are the lancewood tree and native hops.

landcare group Community groups, often volunteers, that work to protect and rejuvenate their local environment, using sustainable land management practices.

lore Spiritual, cultural and practical laws that Indigenous people have followed and lived by for millennia. For example, some lores created ways of living in relation with the land and waters to ensure those places would thrive.

mosaic burning A good cultural burn is when the fire does not burn everything and leaves behind a mosaic pattern of burned black areas and fresh green vegetation. This outcome is carefully planned by the fire practitioners before the burn.

no-fire Country/ecosystem In Australia, the Old People didn't burn every ecosystem. For example, much of the wet rainforest and other related systems don't need burning to stay healthy – they are examples of no-fire ecosystems. In fact, most rainforests and fire-sensitive ecosystems will die if they are burned, which is why traditional fire practitioners restrict fire from those areas to care for them.

Old People Older generations of Indigenous people who hold the traditional knowledge that was passed down from the Ancestors. They have the knowledge and skills to care for Country, understand the lores and share the culture of their people with younger generations.

parent tree Tree that grows into being the main tree in the area; also, a large old tree that supports younger trees and vegetation.

reading Country The art of being able to identify the original form of the natural environment. It is also being able to understand the signs and indicators in the seasons, plants, animals, land and seas in a way that defines the time to apply practices to care for the environment and the people. For example, reading the Country to choose the right time to light the right fire.

reconciliation Building and strengthening relationships based on trust and respect between Indigenous peoples and non-Indigenous peoples. The reconciliation process in Australia acknowledges the colonial history of violence and land dispossession, and the racism that continues today. Groups such as Reconciliation Australia and Reconciliation Action Plans (RAPs) contribute to the reconciliation process.

ringbark A ring of bark is removed from around a tree trunk, with the intention of eventually killing the tree.

saltwater people Indigenous people whose Country is on the coast, where the land meets the sea.

spot-overs, spot-over fires Fires that jump the firebreak created by fire practitioners; if not extinguished, spot-over fires would burn the land the practitioners were trying to save.

story place Area of cultural significance that has been cared for with traditional management practices for millennia. Some story places were only for men, some only for women, some could not be used for hunting or visited at all, and some were areas where everybody could visit, hunt and dwell.

swag A roll or sack made of waterproof material that holds bedding and other belongings; rolled tightly, then tied and slung by a strap across your back, a swag is easy to carry.

tea-tree Also called paperback tree; endemic to Australia, it can grow up to 7 metres tall and is known for its papery white bark. The leaves are rich in oil that is used today for medical and other purposes.

Traditional Custodians/Owners Indigenous people who have cultural ties to particular areas of land and custodial responsibilities for that Country. This responsibility is passed down through the generations from the Ancestors.

understorey Lower-level vegetation in a forest, growing under the tree canopy; also called 'undergrowth'.

Voice to Parliament A permanent body enshrined in the Australian Constitution to make representation to the Australian Parliament and the Executive Government on legislation and policy of significance to Aboriginal and Torres Strait Islander peoples. The First Nations Voice was proposed in the Uluṟu Statement from the Heart in 2017; the 2023 referendum to enshrine the Voice in the Constitution was unsuccessful.

wildfires Also called 'bushfires' in Australia, these are hot fires that create thick, black smoke. Often these severe fire events can lead to the destruction of the natural and built environment and loss of lives, both human and animal.

Conversion table

Metric	**Imperial**
1 millimetre	0.039 inch
1 centimetre	0.394 inch
1 metre	3.28 feet
1 kilometre	0.621 mile
1 hectare	2.47 acres
10 degrees Celsius	50 degrees Fahrenheit

INTRODUCTION

It was the beginning of 2021, and we had enjoyed a beautiful day doing cultural burns with the Traditional Custodians of red sand Country in Central Queensland, Australia. In the same way that our Ancestors have done for centuries, we lit gentle fires that calmly trickled across the rugged landscape in various directions.

We had chosen to burn in the middle of the wet season because the land was choked up with dangerous fuel loads of dead grass that could lead to out-of-control wildfires. The timing had to be perfect to apply the healing fire to improve the poor condition of the land. It didn't take an expert to see that the Country was suffering from more than a hundred years of overgrazing livestock and mismanagement.

We watched as flames danced around a mosaic of red, black and green. The red was the fire doing its work of restoring the land, the patches of black were where the fire had been, while the green patches were unburned grasses and other vegetation that were vibrant and fresh from the recent rains. Every single blade of grass burning had been carefully mapped out beforehand, providing safe areas for wildlife to escape. And having worked with fire for some time now, I knew exactly where each fire would start and where it would go out. We could feel our spirits recharge as we watched the gift of fire – the right sort of fire – elegantly unfold before us, giving back to the landscape.

After the burns, I found myself standing alongside an old friend and colleague at the base of a sandstone escarpment. Our eyes went to a large flat rock that was sticking out and we climbed up onto it. When we reached the top, we were blessed with an amazing view of stoney ironbark Country that blended into the colours of the sunset sky. (Ironbark trees are members of the eucalyptus family.) There was no mobile phone coverage out this way, and I'm always happy to be remote and uncontactable. I stood on the rock, taking it all in, reminding myself how special it is to be connected to the land. Within minutes, the low rumble of an off-road buggy started to compete with the land's peaceful sounds. It was one of the Traditional Owners we had been burning with, coming to find us.

We watched the buggy approach. The driver noticed us standing high on our perch and looked up at us, glowing with the biggest smile. It was her first fire and what she was experiencing brought joy to her spirit. She parked the four-wheeler and scrambled up the rocky slopes to join us. Her eyes feasted on the amazing view and then she gave a cheeky chuckle.

'Look at this, brother, just look at how beautiful that is,' she said, waving her hand around.

'This is what it is all about, aye,' I replied. 'This is the moment that rewards us and Country the most.'

She looked at me with her big, bright eyes and responded with a proud smile. 'True that, brother, aye.'

As the sun set deep into the hills, we headed to camp, where families were preparing dinner. Everyone was busy chipping in and discussing the magical day we had just experienced. The Traditional Owners had been learning cultural fire knowledge on their Country for the first time and a buzz of positive energy filled the evening air. Later we sat by the campfire to tell stories about Country and how important it is for the future of our world. The conversation moved from fire to water, to health, economics and education, and then onto possibilities as endless as the big starry sky that blanketed us.

One of the campers asked how things were going since I wrote my first book, *Fire Country*, in 2020. It is a story about Indigenous fire knowledge and how it may help prevent the disastrous repercussions of wildfires. I said I was happy that *Fire Country* had been well received by people from different walks of life. Writing it had given me the chance to acknowledge mentors from my early years and tell people about the adventures we had putting fire back on Country. It was great to see how a story about traditional knowledge of the land could have such a positive impact. For many people frustrated with the growing number of wildfires across Australia, the book was like a call to arms, a case for considering what Indigenous knowledge has to offer all Australians.

I'd received a few phone calls from non-Indigenous Australians who were interested in what they had read in *Fire Country.*

They told me how upset they were by the destruction caused by wildfires over the decades and still to this day. 'What is wrong with the government?', 'Why don't politicians listen to the Indigenous people from this country?', 'Aboriginal people have lived with fire on this land for thousands of years and the governments still don't listen', were some of their comments. The sweetest response was from a dear old lady who wanted to help and sent me two dollars in the mail. These words and actions brought out the true beauty of humanity.

There is so much to learn from Indigenous knowledge and how it can advance our modern world. After all, there's a reason that Aboriginal stewardship practices such as cultural fire have survived for thousands of years. And when they are given the opportunity to be implemented, they continue to be just as effective today. These ancient practices have their foundations in working together *with* nature, instead of against it. Through my travels, I've discovered that Indigenous communities in North America, Europe and the South Pacific all share this approach of humans working together with nature. Unfortunately, many Elders have passed without being heard, resulting in a loss of knowledge globally and preventing Indigenous knowledge from having the chance to fully demonstrate its worth.

What is most troubling is that modern humanity has disconnected itself from Mother Nature. The colonised structures that control our world have led us to linear ways of thinking. Modern solutions to wildfires are often solely focused on protecting life and property, and while these are important, the exclusion of other considerations have led to a spiralling decline in the health of our planet. Mother Nature is seen as a threat to society, and we end up fighting against nature rather than working with her to uncover universal solutions. Societies become fearful of natural elements, rather than accepting a cultural responsibility of custodianship of our Earth.

When I finished answering questions about my book, there was a moment of silence while I poked the campfire with a stick to encourage the flames. The fire lit up the faces of the other campers as they sat in thought, and then someone said, 'Do you think people are finally listening now that those big wildfires have happened all over the world?' It was almost a year since the 2020 wildfires had ripped through the south-east coast of Australia. Since then, there have been catastrophic infernos in Canada, Greece, Brazil, Hawaii, the United States, and other countries. Yet truthfully, very little has changed in the way societies respond to natural disasters.

So much land has been destroyed, along with huge losses of plants and animals, and that devastation continues every day. Mother Nature has been tirelessly sending warning signs for years, calling out for people to implement change. It's a cry that seems to be getting louder, only to fall upon the deaf ears of governments and business leaders, despite the urgency of her condition.

The only way forward is to start listening to the planet, to realign with nature. This is where traditional knowledge can help. After all, original knowledge systems have been gifted to the First Peoples from Mother Earth herself, based on a relationship of stewardship and respect. Unlike the modern, linear approach, our nature-based solutions offer benefits for both people *and* Country. For some, this approach may be difficult to understand, but now is the time to demonstrate what reconnecting with nature can look like.

No matter how far into the future we go, nature will always be the foundation of our existence. Otherwise, we will become the cause of our own extinction. The greatest achievement of humankind before colonisation was to live on the planet for thousands of generations without destroying it. The challenge for humanity today is to move closer to those ancient perspectives of being connected with nature, especially if we are going to live on the Earth for thousands more years.

'You need to write another story,' said one of the young men. There was another moment of silence as we stared into the firelight. 'There is much more to share that is so important and fascinating beyond our dreams.'

The modern world is yet to understand the magic of connecting with Country and aligning to Mother Earth. Let's continue to talk about traditional knowledge that can – crucially – help heal our planet.

The Knowledge is about reviving Indigenous knowledge across the world. I hope my stories reveal a positive pathway to our uncertain future, a reminder of our place within the natural world. This knowledge is far greater than any one culture or creed; it is bigger than any one person, race, government or agency of any kind. The solutions to ensure the future of humanity and the planet come from the knowledge of creation itself.

CHAPTER 1

The wave for change

As catastrophic wildfires, climate disasters and rapid environmental decline increase across the globe, many people are starting to realise that change is inevitable. We cannot continue to ignore the impact of these events because they are tied directly to our way of life. But changing the way we live with the planet and each other is proving difficult due to the fractured society we have become.

After the terrifying fires of 2019–2020 in Australia, I thought that Aboriginal fire practices were finally going to be accepted. The call for change on a national scale created a hopeful energy that felt empowering and positive. The thirst for fire knowledge seemed to spread as fast as a wildfire itself, and the media was ready to cover anything and everything about Aboriginal burning techniques. Soon, wave after wave of filmmakers and podcasters from many countries were coming to Australia to buy in on the story. I had never experienced anything like it before in the Aboriginal fire space. It was gratifying to see so many people interested in helping to share the message for change. With such a massive public response, it wasn't long before I was inundated with requests and demands for information about cultural burning.

Phone calls and emails came crashing into my communications from people from all over the world. Agencies and community landcare groups sent requests for me to support their attempts to get projects and conferences happening. The will of the people was super charged, and as nice as it was to be flooded with all this interest, it wasn't long before it started to wear me out. Nevertheless, excitement was in the air, and I could visualise ways to bring various groups together to support new, improved cultural-burn programs.

The impact of the wildfires had created a momentum that could possibly take the Aboriginal fire movement to another level. I thought that perhaps cultural burning might actually happen at a government level now, even though there hadn't been much interest politically in the past. But soon the familiar stench of uncertainty blew in, where important issues that are raised today are completely forgotten tomorrow. I wasn't sure how governments could implement traditional fire practices when the politicians didn't know what they were.

In February 2020, the Australian Government launched the Royal Commission into National Natural Disaster Arrangements. It felt like the same old routine, or maybe it was a way to stall things for a while, to allow people time to recover from their fears and frustrations after the fires. To my surprise, an invitation arrived for me to give evidence. It would be my first gig with a royal commission and I didn't know what to expect. It was good to be invited and I hoped it would help support the cause.

Walking into the court on the first day, it looked just like any courtroom you see on television. Shiny desks with little microphones and name tags neatly placed in front of each speaker. Up the front were the main commissioner fellas themselves, sitting in their chairs, ready to enforce order. I had been thinking long and hard about what to say, as I was ready to offer my ten cents worth for the record. The first questions led me to talk about the state of the landscape in terms of vegetation. Then came a couple of the usual questions about what cultural fire is and how it is different from hazard reduction burns. In Australia, hazard reduction burns are lit and managed by rural fire services and other agencies to reduce the severity of bushfires that might occur in the future. I explained how Indigenous fire methods are culturally complex because they aim to help the environment to thrive, rather than solely to protect life and property. When the opportunity came, I began to talk about the possibilities of implementing traditional knowledge solutions. Before I could finish my first sentence, though, I was interrupted by the boss man of the courtroom.

'I am sorry, Mr Steffensen, but you only have to answer the questions that we ask you.'

Then I was told that there was no time left and the session was over. They had asked me to fly across the country to give evidence, but it was only to respond to the questions they wanted to ask. I walked out feeling unheard, even though a lot of information had been shared that could have led to something constructive. I knew that nothing out of the ordinary was going to happen, not in a hurry anyway. It was now in the hands of the legislative system that had helped to get us into this mess in the first place.

In the final report of the royal commission, published in October 2020, Aboriginal fire practices were strongly recommended but, as always, they weren't taken seriously. The fire management agencies were not doing much to bring Indigenous expertise to the round-table discussions. So, I wasn't optimistic that the ways agencies and governments manage the land with fire would change. Announcements about better evacuation plans and more hazard reduction burns were made across the country, putting on steroids what hadn't worked well in the past, rather than understanding how to do things differently into the future.

Panels of Western scientists declared that climate change was to blame. They said there was no form of fire management that could have saved Australia from such devastating wildfires. This talk about the doomed days of climate change only pumped more fear and uncertainty into the situation. 'It's climate change; there is nothing we can do.' The Western experts made this claim with no understanding of the original fire knowledge of the land and without giving First Nations people the chance to prove otherwise. It was clear that their knowledge had come from their experiences of fighting fires the Western way. And in our modern society where people know very little about the land, their statements were quickly and dangerously accepted. Pointing the finger at Mother Nature alone is far easier than examining our own wrongdoings. I will talk about climate change later in the book, and there are references in *Fire Country* that also explore this issue.

From the day the British hit the shores of what's now called Botany Bay in Sydney, much of Australia's vast landscape has not been properly managed with fire. The impact of colonisation still contributes to the land's declining health, which makes nature vulnerable to unprecedented threats. Many of the areas in New South Wales devastated by wildfires in 2019–2020 were also hit almost 40 years earlier, and although a combination of drought and heavy wind conditions fiercely fuelled those infernos, since colonisation the land has not been kept in a state of preparedness. The same mistakes were made over again, as people continued to neglect the land to create time bombs of fuel loads waiting to go off. The further we venture into the future with this destructive behaviour, the worse these repetitive threats will become to our way of life. We seriously need new approaches from leaders who know how to listen and think outside the box. Like this quote often attributed to Einstein says: 'You can't solve a problem with the same mindset that created it.' But tell that to those people in power who won't allow space for a different way of thinking. It's as if there is a dark cloud hanging over us, but we are not looking up to see it.

The Australian wildfires helped trigger a national political debate about the burning of fossil fuels versus renewable energy. The left wing is screaming that climate change induced by humans is the cause of extreme weather events, while the right wing is saying that wildfires are a natural part of life in Australia. There is some truth in these different claims, but so often the politicians argue from their party's agendas. The left and right sides of the Western political divide will debate the situation to the point of hopelessness. Meanwhile, the optimism that wildfires will be addressed through traditional knowledge solutions fades.

Following the 2019–2020 fires, I was invited onto one of Australia's national television news programs to talk about the wildfires from the traditional knowledge background. It seemed like a good thing to do because the topic was important and cultural fire needed to be represented. The first question the host asked me was about blaming the fires on poor land management.

I agreed with that and went on to explain why poor land management is making the nation more receptive to wildfires, with the land becoming drier and more vulnerable. Then I mentioned that modern-day Australia is not skilled to manage the land the way Aboriginal people have done for tens of thousands of years.

The news man looked pleased with my answer and, live on air, he gave credit to Aboriginal fire knowledge. Then he made another point in a way that seemed to assume I would agree: 'It's obvious that it is bad land management, Victor. It certainly doesn't have anything to do with climate change, that's for sure.' Before he went on, I cut in to disagree. I said that we can't ignore that we are burning too much fossil fuel and over-extracting from the earth. We can't separate the problem of polluting our atmosphere with greenhouse emissions from the fact that we are destroying our Country with bad land management. Both sides of the argument need to be dealt with together.

After I made that statement, the interview came to an end and the show was over. When I tried to find a recording of the program on the internet, there was no trace of the interview. It was clear that it had been crafted solely to target the bad land management side of the story. They simply wanted to attack the environmentalist political party for their land management policies, while taking attention away from climate change and the impact of mining coal and gas. The interviewer had tried to lead me into the argument between the left and right, and I wanted no part of it. After that encounter I became wary of doing other interviews with the national news networks.

At this time, many non-Indigenous organisations realised that Aboriginal fire practices could lead to big opportunities for them. Some agencies tried to employ Aboriginal people to drive their cultural fire programs, but many of these people quit because the programs ended up being Western fire management dressed up as cultural burning. Sometimes agencies would call it a cultural burn just because they had an Aboriginal fella there on the day, regardless of their fire knowledge. Ticking the box of Indigenous engagement was where most agency attempts stopped; their only aim was to satisfy the bureaucratic requirements.

Everyone was using the term 'cultural burning', whether or not they knew what they were talking about. In some cases, it became like a commodity, with individuals looking at ways to benefit from it, rather than taking a community approach. The whole intention of sharing knowledge and stewardship is for individuals and groups to work strongly together, instead of falling into the pit of competitiveness. I quickly learned that loyalty and collaboration are very scarce in a world full of greed.

Following the recommendations of the royal commission, the Australian Government made substantial funding available to Indigenous groups. For the not-for-profit organisation I co-founded, then called Firesticks, this was one of the few times we received government funding to support a network of communities. The money was helpful, but I saw it as a band-aid solution and it was not what I was hoping for. Receiving funding on its own didn't mean we could do useful work when outdated Western land management policies continued to stand in the way. I would have preferred the more tangible outcome of creating partnerships with land management agencies, wildfire services, councils and communities.

What I truly hope is for politicians to support cultural fire practices as a service to their nation. Giving money to try to solve an issue is a wasted opportunity if it is not accompanied by a strategic, collaborative plan that leads to real, responsible and ongoing action. I have found that usually the funding dries up in two years or so. Then you have to fulfil the same old reporting requirements and worry about what will happen next. It feels as if some groups are set up to fail because many of the government requirements around funding and policies are very complicated and difficult for Indigenous communities to manage.

Two years after the wildfires in Australia, on their election in May 2022, the new federal Labor Government announced the proposal for an Indigenous Voice to Parliament. The whole nation would have the opportunity in October 2023 to vote Yes or No in a referendum for the recognition of Indigenous people in the Australian Constitution. The campaign created a huge divide that led us all to go backwards. It was a disastrous political debate, filled with conspiracies, and it brought out the bad side of an ill-conditioned society. For me, it was disappointing to see racism openly displayed across our nation; one of the oldest cultures on Earth was treated so badly, for all the world to witness. I didn't want anything to do with the referendum because it felt politically demoralising from both the Yes and No sides of the debate.

Having an Indigenous Voice that contributes to positive solutions to take care of community and Country would be amazing. That's all I'd hoped for before this campaign made its mark on our history, and will hope for in the future. Yet there were claims that Aboriginal people were going to take over the land, steal non-Indigenous Australians' property, force citizens to pay rent taxes. Seeing the way the nation behaved on the matter made me sad, as I realised that we still have a long way to go. I did not want the good work of healing community and Country caught up in this political mud fight.

The strong support for cultural fire practices following the wildfires was now dead in the wind. The No campaign had turned it into a conspiracy, projecting fear that these practices were part of a strategy to take over the nation. Trying to save our environment and help improve the lives of all future generations was now an evil plan. I tried to prevent our organisation from being involved in this political mess, to protect the integrity of our Old People's knowledge, but that was hard to achieve.

In 2023, I was involved in creating a carbon-credit-like initiative through Firesticks in collaboration with our partners. We were developing a campaign to raise money to help Indigenous communities implement traditional fire and land management programs, create jobs for people to carry out these programs, and buy the equipment needed for regions to heal the land. We were aiming to encourage positive change, moving our communities towards autonomy, which is where they need to be. There were billboards at airports to advertise the credits, and it was exciting to get the message out there so that the nation could contribute. This was in the early stages of the initiative, and we were keen to see how the advertising campaign would work and what we could learn from it to develop better models for the cause. Then the same TV network that had interviewed me about the wildfires contacted me again. This time the call came from a radio presenter, who invited me to be interviewed on their show.

I thought it was going to be an intelligent conversation about the fire-credits scheme and its design to support a not-for-profit initiative to care for Country. So I agreed. As soon as the interview started, the presenter attacked the goodwill we were trying to share. He asked where the money would go, as if it was being pocketed by scammers. Then he downgraded traditional knowledge by saying that it wasn't supported by science and that he wanted a professional opinion on the matter. I realised that he was trying to undermine our scheme and answered the questions in a way that kept him honest every time. But no matter how much truth I injected into the conversation, his attitude did not change. It reached the point where I raised my voice to take the upper hand, but the presenter cut me off and ended the segment.

Afterwards, listening to him talk to the audience members who called in was demoralising. His comments about our fire-credits program were disrespectful and he clearly tied it to what he chose to believe was a conspiracy of the Yes campaign for the Voice referendum. 'Why do we need a Voice when we have Aboriginal organisations already profiting?' Then one of the radio station workers came onto the phone to thank me for the interview. 'Thanks for doing that. I just want to let you know that you are a good person and that you are doing great work,' they said. 'Yeah, thanks,' I replied.

I later saw the interview posted on social media. The host had thrown it out there for his listeners to make critical comments. 'It's a scam', 'The gravy train rides again', 'Money for nothing, as usual', and even more vile responses that you would not want to read. These comments served the network's hateful campaign well and all I could do was tell myself that it was part of the sickness of conspiracies and misinformation. Then a television news program on the same network aired a story about the fire-credit conspiracy that was instigated by the radio interview. They did not do any research into the matter at all, just put it out there as a scam, without inviting me on air to challenge their lies. A sucker punch to the cultural burning programs and Aboriginal people broadcast openly on television news. It seems that the media networks are allowed to manipulate information to suit their political agendas.

The worst part is that a large section of society believes these misconceptions. It is hard to heal relations between people when public media platforms are promoting misleading information. Just as an ancient forest takes so long to recover after being damaged by a catastrophic event, it can take time for conspiracy theories to be replaced with truth. Our entire society is riddled with manipulative complications fuelled by competing agendas. This can foster negativity between all community groups in our society, disconnecting people from each other.

If people do not work together, nothing ever gets done and everyone loses, as does Country. It's often a problem based on greed, and that can have dangerous consequences. Instead, we could be working together to heal the planet. If it's bad behaviour that has caused the damage to the land, then it makes sense to focus on improving our attitudes as a crucial starting point to save it. This is undoubtedly possible because we have the power of Mother Nature on our side, if we are wise enough to realise it.

Like gasping for air to stay alive, we need to reconnect with each other and the planet. That is why traditional knowledge formed by timeless cultural connections to the Earth can help modern society to restore our fundamental values. I am not talking about protecting nationalistic values through the wars and fighting that have made their mark on all human histories. Rather, that we have the opportunity to grasp onto the deep knowledge and connection many ancient nations have had with nature from the very beginning. That is the gem we have the opportunity to uncover and hold fast.

When the first settlers came to Australia, they regarded the people they called 'natives' as primitive when judged against their own civilisation. The smoke screen of having very little clothing and living off the land fooled the Europeans into thinking there was nothing to learn from the Aboriginal people. This portrait is still within the thinking of modern society. Uneducated critics still claim that Aboriginal people didn't invent anything except rubbing two sticks together to make fire.

The Aboriginal understanding of the natural world holds so many secrets to achieving prosperity and it has been totally overlooked to this day. Many non-Indigenous people still see the land and Indigenous people in the same light as the first settlers did centuries ago, as primitive and of no use to our modern society. But we will not flourish when the majority of people in the twenty-first century are disconnected from nature. No matter how well advanced we believe we are, if we are not aligned with natural lore then we will continue to see a drastic decline in the health of the land and of our society. The alternative is for modern society to connect with nature in the ways that Indigenous people have done for millennia. Of course, this may not mean roaming the land wearing little clothing and living the traditional lifestyle of the Ancestors. But it will require the same connection and values, combined with our evolving technologies and modern lifestyles.

Many believe that Indigenous people need help to fit into the material world, or that only the privileged are successful members of society, while the disadvantaged have to catch up with them. But in reality, no one culture is perfect in the times we share today. Equally, every culture around the globe has important knowledge that can help to restore the health of the world. Understanding this is crucial if we are going to work together in a more mature way, rather than continuing practices that leave Mother Nature vulnerable. The land, seas and universe can guide us and, in turn, be the first beneficiaries of our actions.

We still have a long way to go, but people are slowly becoming aware of cultural fire and land management practices in mainstream society. These practices can be effective within any space, as long as they are based on the ways traditional knowledge is integrated with nature. The method is simple: less talk and more listening combined with practical action to lead the way forward, as well as working with the entire community to learn a different way of practically caring for the land. The more we involve people in this work, the more we will achieve positive outcomes. We need to change the practices and mindsets that have destroyed so much in our recent past and collaborate with all stakeholders to build people's capacity to care for the land.

When we use old practices to work with the land, it will generally respond positively and good outcomes can be achieved. The more we produce this truth from the land, the wiser we will become, and that leads to improving our way of thinking. I have seen non-Indigenous people who fear fire turn into the greatest advocates for cultural burning, and divided communities finally working together, simply through a shared understanding of Country. I've also seen troubled Indigenous youth find rehabilitation through restoring their culture. The list of these positive transitions goes on and the interest in new endeavours continues to grow. Working with Indigenous knowledge can lead to better outcomes for the environment, culturally connect people with the land and improve livelihoods. Then everyone can see themselves as part of the planet and show respect for people and place no matter what their origin across the world. Whether you are aware of it or not, Mother Nature has already thrown us into this wave for change by increasing extreme weather patterns and through threats of environmental decline. Hopefully we will not crash down to be wrecked on the rocky shores of uncertainty.

We can give traditional knowledge the chance to restore a thriving planet. This has proven extremely challenging in the recent histories of Western societies, though. When it comes to accepting solutions for change based on traditional knowledge, we must overcome fear-based conspiracies that will only kill opportunity. These solutions are often seen as a threat to the privileged elites in society. Many people refuse to listen to advice that challenges their current beliefs, let alone adopt practices drawn from traditional knowledge. I find it mind blowing how self-limiting we have collectively become as a society, and this is causing serious damage to the natural world. It is a problem greater than all the natural disasters combined, because it is the condition of our society that has created those disasters in the first place. Humans are originally a product of nature, but the laws that govern our society are not.

It is useful to look at the systems that created divisions between people, which have stopped them from accepting traditional knowledge. Throughout Western history, so much pain has been inflicted through colonisation. The victims have always been the powerless minorities, left to suffer the intergenerational trauma of disadvantage. Although we still see minorities being treated poorly, events are occurring where people and governments are beginning to pay for the injustices of the past.

The mistreatment of our environment is threatening our water quality and food production, leading to native plant and animal extinction, and restricting the freedom our forefathers had to live on the land, to name but a few of the consequences. In Australia, these are the long-term results of changes the colonisers brought to this land. We are now all experiencing the same problems across the world, which means we need to share the same solutions.

A challenging place to begin is to accept that we are in this situation together, regardless of our differences. We have a collective mindset that has been conditioned by colonisation and it doesn't discriminate between culture or creed. It may help us to acknowledge that if we are not living in harmony with Mother Nature, then we are not in harmony with each other.

As well as the practice of cultural fire, there are so many other insights drawn from traditional knowledge that can improve social and environmental wellbeing. Cultural fire practices have been the spearhead to demonstrate how old knowledge can influence solutions in the modern world. It is possible to draw on this knowledge and work on healing ourselves, so we can take on the task of healing our beautiful planet.

CHAPTER 2

Fighting fire with traditional knowledge

For tens of thousands of years, Aboriginal people managed the land with cool fires to avoid wildfires from destroying the natural resources that supported them. In fire-sensitive Country, they kept the land healthy without fire. This sophisticated form of land care is a proactive approach to applying fire when and where it is needed to ensure biodiversity health, which is the clear difference between Indigenous and Western fire cultures.

The Old People taught us that every plant species responds to heat in its own way. These various responses contribute to creating the great diversity of ecosystems that we see in Australia and in other countries. That is also why Indigenous fire methods are used to burn different vegetation types at specific times of the year. In Australia, thousands of years of Aboriginal burning has assisted native plants to evolve and respond to fire this way. Fire practitioners learn to recognise this complexity and make decisions about ways to apply fire depending on the identity of Country, and that learning takes time.

Reinstating logical, proactive, long-term solutions such as cultural burning has not been properly established in recent times. Western ways have taken charge over the past few generations, making it close to impossible to carry out cultural burns. Modern firefighting sits in the arena of paramilitary-like operations in a new world of liability and legislation. It is a Westernised industry that responds to disasters and serves a broader culture that fears fire. When mixed with bureaucracy and egos, there is little opportunity to influence general perceptions through the Indigenous lens. The main aims of Western firefighting practices are safety and to protect life and property.

While it is important to have firefighters deployed to achieve these goals, there is also a desperate need for a parallel workforce of land and fire practitioners to focus on caring for Country. Fire practitioners who use very different strategies from the prescribed hazard reduction fires we see today. Working to limit the effects of wildfires by restoring nature's identity will be ongoing for generations, but it is the ultimate solution with the greatest rewards.

When it comes to controlling fires, I always remember the day a dear Elder and mentor broke off a branch from an ironwood tree, which grows in Cooktown in North Queensland. 'This is what the Old People used to put the fire out in the olden days,' he said, holding the leafy branch in his hand and giving me the biggest smile. We were burning Country at the time, and the Old Man started to walk along the edge of the fire line, sweeping the fire back onto itself with the branch. He swung it around and around, keeping the momentum of the swing to a perfect circle as he whipped the ground, flicking out the fire.

Swinging the branch this way made the job effortless, and it was enjoyable to watch how it was done the old way. It looked like the Elder was performing a traditional dance as he waddled along the fire's edge without breaking the style of the swing. 'This ironwood is the best one to use because the leaves don't fall off when you hit the ground,' he said in his high, happy tone. There were other trees that were good for the job but that was the preferred one for his Country. The Old Man explained that they would burn places to clear the grass to make a camp and then put the flames out again. As well as being used to put out the fire, the branches also made a good broom to sweep the ground clean for camping.

Understanding Country through the lens of traditional knowledge could help us to make safer decisions. The Old Man taught me safe ways of back-burning to stop wildfires. While back-burning is well known in Western ways of fighting fire, the Aboriginal version is more aligned with reading the land, which makes it very effective. It allows practitioners to make accurate decisions to back-burn in areas that are not so flammable and are easier to control, especially in hot and dry conditions. This knowledge could also help us to find the best place to escape to safety if things ever did go pear-shaped on the fire front.

Understanding how fire behaves across different vegetation types and seasons is an advantage when deciding where to back-burn in the best way possible. Uneducated guesses about back-burning can create more devastating fire fronts that only worsen the situation. Unnecessary back-burning has certainly occurred during some of the recent wildfires in Australia, but it rarely gets mentioned in the media. In some cases, the main fire front would never have reached certain places, but they were set alight anyway from panic. Overall, it is fair to say that the fear of wind change is the main driver to undertaking difficult decisions.

Early one Sunday morning a phone call came asking me to help fight a wildfire that had started in a national park. I had been watching the raging fire on the television news over the past couple of weeks.

'When do you want me to come down?' I asked.

'We can book your flight to come down immediately,' was the reply.

I had just got home from doing a fire workshop the day before, but this was important enough to sacrifice the weekend.

The Traditional Owners of the Country had called me and that was the only way I would be invited to take part in such an operation. The Aboriginal staff employed by the agency were keen to prevent their traditional lands from being incinerated. The fire had destroyed so much land over the last couple of weeks, and it could take out the whole region if it wasn't stopped. The non-Indigenous park rangers worked well with the Aboriginal staff, which meant we had a good ground crew. When I arrived, they gave me a warm welcome and then we got down to the job.

The first thing was to head to the fire front and assess the situation. I jumped in a four-wheel drive with two of the Aboriginal rangers and we drove out on the rugged sandy roads.

Two other Aboriginal rangers in another firefighting vehicle came to assist us. We carefully checked the unburned terrain a few kilometres before the fire front, which was yet to receive the brunt of the inferno. While we were there, we had the job of protecting some cultural sites that the community was concerned about. To help with the situation, National Parks sent out a contractor with a small bulldozer to put firebreaks around the sites.

One of the Traditional Owners instructed the dozer driver to make a firebreak around the special areas, which was only a small parcel of land. We continued towards the fire front, and the smoke was starting to show itself through the trees. We crossed a wooden bridge over a small but deep-running creek that was choked up with bullrush and sword grass. The long stalks were swaying in the fast current of the crystal-clear water, which looked like it must be a magical place for fish. The reeds grew thick along the banks that led to a good swamp of tea-trees, which are also called paperbarks. With the fire front so close, there was nothing we could do to save that beautiful place, and those trees were sadly wiped out by the fire later that day.

On the other side of the bridge was a large system of dry rainforest Country that had lots of leaf litter on the ground from its fire-sensitive trees. The dry rainforest system stretched on for a long way, and I could immediately see a missed opportunity. 'We could have stopped the fire here if we'd acted a day or two before,' I said, as we drove along the sandy road.

'I know, cuz, I wish we could have all been here doing this earlier,' replied one of the leading Traditional Owners. I will call him Charlie, although that was not his real name. He was a similar age to me and had some experience working on Country with National Parks. But most of all he was my good brother and friend who I had helped over the years in teaching fire.

He explained that they had tried to back-burn a few times further north in some thick grass Country and the fire got away. 'They waited too long to act, brother, and now the fire is too large and dangerous for them,' he said in a frustrated voice.

The other Indigenous crew member brought our attention to the wooden bridge. 'Them bridges costs thousands of dollars to build. We should save it.'

I looked at the choked-up water reeds, and we agreed to start burning around the structure as best as possible. It is always a mission to burn wetland grasses safely, because even though it is water-based vegetation, it is intensely flammable. While we worked around the bridge the second vehicle went back to check on the sacred areas. As soon as we'd saved the bridge by burning around it, we could hear the others calling in on the two-way radio. They told us to come quickly as the bulldozer had caught on fire.

We took off in our truck and found the crew tending to the mini bulldozer engulfed in flames. They had already pulled the driver out of the blazing machine to safety and had moved him away to recover. He was in a state of shock and his shaking hands were trying to grasp onto his wobbling knees.

'You'll be alright, mate, just keep cool under the shade here,' Charlie said, putting a hand on the guy's shoulder to comfort him. In the meantime, the rest of the crew were pouring water over the dozer to put out the fire before it got away.

I walked back over to inspect the bulldozer, which had been destroyed. 'How did this thing catch on fire? The wildfire's a long way away,' I said to Charlie.

'Brother, look where he is working. He's way too close to the sacred site. We told him to go way over there,' Charlie said, pointing to an area away from the site. 'Them Ancestors must have got angry with him and blew that bulldozer up.'

The driver could have been killed if he hadn't escaped the air-conditioned cabin fast enough.

'Luckily it's a diesel machine, aye,' I said as I looked at the melting dashboard that was still smoking away.

After doing what we could to save that area, Charlie ordered some of the crew to help the driver get into his truck nearby. The next thing on my mind was to assess the land to the south, away from the fire front, to see where we could stop this terrible blaze. Protecting the smaller patches of culturally significant places from the incoming wildfire was the easy part. We had to find ways to stop the main inferno from devastating the whole landscape. Further south of the region was beautiful Country, along with popular tourist hotels and a community that were all in the line of fire. As we drove around the countryside, I didn't see any park rangers out on the fireground to assist us.

'Hey, where are the ranger fellas? Why aren't they out here with us?' I asked Charlie.

'They are not allowed on the fireground at the moment because it is too dangerous,' he shouted, as we drove along.

We continued to assess the area, only to see a suffering, unmanaged landscape full of fuel. It was coastal heath land, which made things worse because that is one of the most flammable types of vegetation. I mentioned how unhealthy and messy the landscape was and Charlie just shook his head. 'Brother, I wish they would listen to us, aye. We should be looking after our own Country our way.'

We studied the different types of ecosystems to find the best area from which to back-burn. Normally, with good fire, we only burn one ecosystem at a time at different times of the year, but in this situation, we had to burn a few ecosystems that were the fastest, safest and easiest to work with. As it was summer, all land types were flammable, so burning a few ecosystems was inevitable when fighting this fire. We needed to find a starting point to burn across the fire zone to the containment lines, which were the waterways and ocean on either side of the region. We searched for the narrowest part of the fire zone that was still available, which was 13 kilometres across. With the local knowledge of Charlie and his crew, we were able to find what we were looking for quite quickly.

The hardest vegetation we eventually chose to burn was at the start of the area, on the far west side. A big swamp that led into waterways, it was full of old dead sword grass that had dangerously built up over the years. I knew that the process of burning it was not going to be much fun; due to its flammable nature it always burns extremely wild and hot. After that we moved onto land that was suppressed with leaf litter, which transitioned up the hill into dry rainforest. The last leg of the back-burn was a forest of tall blackbutt trees that we could get through in the cool hours before dawn. It was the best route to cut off the wildfire and, from the limited options available, it was the only way.

The dry northern winds were moderately strong and continued to push the fire front further south, towards the populated areas. We checked the weather forecast and found that there was going to be a small window for a wind change. The south-easterlies were setting in the next day for 24 hours, which was the only break possible. We had to back-burn all day and night before the strong northerly winds returned to stir up the beast again. We were set on this plan and we needed National Parks to support us, so we went back to base to inform them. The head ranger and the crew were good people and they were keen to hear us out and to support our idea.

'We will have to go through the plan with the Incident Management Team [IMT] in Brisbane to get the operation approved first,' the head ranger said in a supportive way.

'Let's do it,' I said. 'There's no time to waste.'

We sat in the office around the computer and met online with the IMT officer in charge to present our action plan. Charlie and I explained the route and the vegetation we had assessed, which followed roads all the way across the fire zone. We explained why it was safe and that we could work quickly with the support of good ground crews. I hoped that they would see the common sense in the plan, and to my surprise they did without too much hesitation.

It was approved and we quickly agreed to leave first thing in the morning. That was when the favourable change of the south-easterly winds was due to offer its window of opportunity. We met up with the National Park staff involved to discuss the plan. At dawn we were on our way with two fire fighting vehicles and a crew of four. The ranger told me that more help was coming and there were helicopters flying nearby, dumping water on the main fire front, which we could call on.

We arrived at our ignition point and went over the plan with our small but determined crew. I could see that they were working themselves up for the experience, and I knew that was a sign of a dedicated team. We stood there waiting for the approval to come from the IMT officer, who was many kilometres away in the capital city. I asked again if they could send more back-up crew as soon as they could manage.

We needed them to cover our tail while we did the back-burn, just in case there were any spot-overs. Spot-overs are fires that jump the firebreak, and they would burn the land we were trying to save. It would be easy going, as the other side of the firebreak was leaf litter that made any spot-overs start very slow and low. Slow enough to put out any fires quickly before they could flare up and get away. The most frustrating part was waiting for the command from the IMT to get started. It was like waiting for the red light to turn green at a traffic intersection.

'Let's go,' Charlie bellowed, as soon as the IMT officer gave us the green light. We shook hands and lit the first patch of that scary sword grass in the dry wetlands. We had a fair bit to get through before reaching the leaf-litter Country and it was going to be hot, hard work. As soon as I put a flame near that dry water grass it lit up in an instant.

The appropriate style of burning was to not use any drip torches for the first dangerous run of sword-grass Country. We had to go slow and make sure the fire behind us was burned out along the road before we moved on. We did this by lighting one or two spot fires at a time and then waited for them to join up to form a burned edge that created a safe break. As it burned out the edge of the road, I watched the fire go ballistic when it engulfed the thick sword grass deeper into the swamp. Spot fire after spot fire, I moved the back-burn along as the crew behind me put out burning tea-trees that hung above our firebreak.

We had to burn this way because going fast with a drip torch would create a line of fire that would be too difficult, stressful and dangerous for the crew to manage. Not using fossil fuel to light the grass made the fire a little calmer, although the heat coming from the sword grass on that hot summer day was unbearable. We continued lighting spot fires, waiting for the fire to join up and close the gaps, then moving onward as the crew gave me the thumbs-up that all was under control.

Charlie was with me up the front and we put in spot fires that were roughly 2 to 3 metres apart. As we did this, we watched quite a few native mice and bandicoots come running out through the unburned gaps and across the road to safety. Charlie pointed out the native mice running with tiny babies clinging onto their backs. They were hanging onto Mum with their dear little lives, and it was like watching a rodeo as they bucked across the road. If we had used the drip torch, we would have trapped them in the swamp to be burned alive. So many animals are killed by the wrong style of burning, which defeats the purpose of fighting the fire in the first place.

Onwards we went, while I kept my eye on the raging fire we had created deep within the swamp. It was the head of the fire and one change in the wind could make it rush straight at us to jump the line. When the wind started to push the fire along, we would speed up the back-burn to make sure we had the lead in closing it off.

Then the south-east winds turned to short gusts of northerlies again, causing the raging fire deep in the swamp to come charging. We met it with the trusty fire hose to settle things down while we moved along. We only used the water when we really needed it; we had just two fire units, so we had to save the water for sticky situations. After what seemed like an endless battle, I could see the leaf-litter Country not far away. That leafy landscape was a sight for sore eyes, as it burns far slower and lower than sword grass ever will.

When we finally made it past the swamp there was instant relief. It was our first small victory and it helped us to relax for a moment. We would be able to move much faster now and it would be smooth sailing from here. The ranger called in a helicopter to dump some water to help settle down our back-burn fire in the swamp, and it was good to experience this collaboration. We cruised along, burning the leaves, and then Charlie started yelling out in excitement, 'Let's go, my brother, let's go!'

He was happy that we were on our way to stop this wildfire once and for all.

'Yeah, my bro, fair way to go still but we got it now,' I replied.

Further along we went, stopping every now and then to wait for the crew to catch up.

'All good back there, brother!' I yelled out to Charlie.

He looked at me with the biggest smile and said that all was well. 'Keep going, keep going, let's go,' he yelled again.

He started to get proper excited with all the success, so he took his shoes off and began clapping them together like clapsticks.

Next, he started doing a corroboree dance on the sandy road as we poked along with the back-burn. It was a good laugh, and it instantly made the situation more enjoyable. 'I'm gonna keep going barefoot, my brother, cause that's how we roll,' Charlie said, while he danced along the road in his shorts and t-shirt. He felt close to his Ancestors when caring for his Country and looked good with his feet kicking up the sand as he danced against that backdrop of fire and smoke.

I had Crocs shoes on, and I have always worn them for burning Country, but everyone in the government agencies followed their personal protective equipment (PPE) rules and wore work boots. All our Indigenous fire practitioners are encouraged to wear good boots and reasonable work clothes, and they do. It's not that I or other Aboriginal people are ignoring what the authorities recommend should be worn on the fireground. It is simply that we wear what we feel comfortable in, and that is the way it has always been through my life. I think non-Indigenous people are beginning to understand this, because many agencies are relaxing their rules and guidelines now that they can see the nature of the cool burns.

Personally, I find all that protective gear is way too hot and weighs me down, and the big work boots make me clumsy, so I end up tripping over. I can't feel the Country under my feet when I wear them. It makes it harder to work and I can't move quickly through the land to check where the fire is at. I don't intend to be in front of the fire storms when fighting fire, so I don't need a fireproof suit. But most of all, I don't want the Old People's spirits looking down at me wearing that gear on Country. They would have a good laugh, as it goes against everything they ever taught me about fire. We did all our burning barefoot when they were alive and not once did any of us get burned by the fire. We didn't know anything about Western laws back then, as we were not yet tainted by bureaucracy.

As Charlie and I moved the fire along, another National Park vehicle and two staff turned up to give us a hand. We quickly briefed them to check the line to make sure the fire didn't jump across the road. There was a moment or two when the fire burned across the road, but it was no trouble to put it out. If it had been flammable vegetation, they wouldn't have been able to control it in that summer heat.

Looking back from where we'd started, I could see that we had covered some distance and we were going extremely well. The rangers assured us that more support crews were coming, but I was starting to wonder why they weren't there already. It was okay though, because we were moving closer to the dry rainforest Country and that should be the end of the fire threat. But then one of the park rangers received a message we didn't want to hear. The IMT officer in charge 300 kilometres away said a spot-over had jumped our break and had created a fire 5 kilometres south of us.

'How can we have a spot-over to the south while the wind is blowing north in the same direction we are burning? That's impossible,' I said. 'Is it from our fire?'

The ranger looked confused and said that it was reported from our fire. Immediately, Charlie and I jumped into the truck to go find this spot-over. We drove up to a high point where we could see the unburned landscape behind us. There was no spot-over to be seen. We drove further south to make sure, until we came to a river that confirmed that the coast was clear.

When we returned, we told our park ranger colleague that there was no spot-over 5 kilometres south. He had to have the incident cleared by the IMT officer in charge, so we stood aside waiting for their approval to continue the mission. Minutes went by and then we heard a helicopter coming our way to inspect around our back-burn area.

We looked up to see some park rangers scoping the area, including the ranger in charge of the park who was assisting us from the local ranger base. She radioed down to say that it was a beautiful back-burn. I watched the chopper swing off to the south to scope the area and they came back reporting no spot-over. In my mind, that was all the confirmation we needed to carry on.

'Let's go, we've wasted enough time,' I yelled, feeling confident again. But the ranger on the ground with us was still trying to get the all-clear from the IMT officer far away.

Charlie was also waiting in anticipation as the delay had wasted almost an hour of our time. At that moment the park ranger walked over to us with his head hanging towards the ground. 'I'm really sorry, but we have just been ordered to stop burning and go back to base.'

Charlie and I looked at our ranger friend in disbelief. Why would they make that decision? We'd had it confirmed on land and in the air that there was no spot-over and our burn was going well.

'I'm so embarrassed that this has happened. I'm really sorry,' he said.

I wanted to keep going anyway, but the ranger explained that if we did, he would lose his job. As I stood there, I came to realise that the burn was officially over and that made me furious. We were so close to stopping this fire only to be told to leave by someone we could not see, let alone could reason with. I later heard that the officer in charge who'd approved our plan had changed shift and the next one didn't like what he saw.

There was no other option but to leave, so Charlie drove me out, both of us upset with what had happened. On the way back to base, we saw a huge fleet of National Park vehicles heading towards the fire front. One after another from various districts around the state. Charlie insisted we stop and talk to the driver of the leading car who was in charge of the convoy.

'What are you fellas doing?' Charlie asked the man, who he knew.

The ranger didn't answer clearly but basically told us they were going to back-burn to stop the fire. I was both shocked and humiliated, which made me even angrier. All we could do was advise them to keep following the fire trail we'd been on and continue where we left off.

'No worries,' the driver said, and then he drove off like the Pied Piper with his long line of firefighting vehicles following behind.

You can imagine what Charlie and I were saying as we drove out of that place.

Within the hour I was in a nearby coastal town in a sports club, having some food and a rest. My flight was booked and I just needed to kill a little time before heading back home, away from this catastrophe. While sitting at a table, looking out the window, I could see a smoke plume in the far distance rising from the exact area where we had been back-burning.

By the geography of the hills, I noticed that it was way further south than our planned route to cut off the wildfire. I phoned Charlie to check, and he said they had started a new back-burn 5 kilometres south from our fire line.

'Yeah, brother,' he said wearily. 'That's them fellas we passed, back-burning from that river we drove along earlier.'

'That area is choked up with tea-tree over their heads. They will never back-burn through that stuff in this heat,' I replied. The National Park crews were starting all over again instead of continuing from where we had created a huge head start.

'I know, brother. There is nothing we can do now except let them go,' Charlie said, sounding very disappointed.

I ended the call and watched the massive plume of black smoke fill the sky. The news came a little later that they lost control of that back-burn within the first hour and had to evacuate. All I could do was sit dumbfounded and shake my head, thinking about what I'd just experienced. It was clear to me that the Western firefighters on this occasion did not know the land and that was what had made things even more dangerous for them.

On my way home, my head was filled with questions about the whole situation. Why didn't the IMT officer in charge talk to me directly to find out what we were doing? Why didn't he listen to his own staff, who reported that there was no spot-over? Why did they send a whole convoy of rangers out to execute a plan without our team knowing anything about it? Why didn't they support our plan, which the first IMT officer in charge had approved? There had to be sensible answers to at least some of those questions, but to this day I still haven't heard any.

Maybe the answers come from some firefighting policy, or maybe they have nothing to do with firefighting at all.

A month or two later I received a phone call from some government workers who were gathering evidence for an enquiry into that wildfire. They asked if I could give some insights onto why the fire happened the way it did.

'We know that you were not there fighting the fire, but we want to interview you anyway, due to your knowledge of fire and environment,' one man said.

When I told him that I had the opportunity to fight that fire at one stage during the event, he and the others were shocked.

'You were there?' he said. 'No one told us that during our investigations.'

I sat down and put my mobile phone onto loudspeaker to get comfortable for the conversation. It felt a bit disappointing to be shoved under the carpet but at the same time it was not surprising that they didn't know I had been there. 'Grab a cup of tea,' I said to the investigation team on the other end of the line. 'I will tell you what happened from my understanding.'

They noted down everything I said, and I could feel the frustration coming from them as the story rolled along. From their incident report, the conclusion was that negligence of some kind contributed to the situation. I was glad that they didn't blame it solely on climate change for once. Instead, they laid it on the way people managed the land and how they responded to the wildfire.

Two years later I had the opportunity to go back to that place. Charlie greeted me together with a couple of other practitioners who ran an Indigenous fire-mentorship program in their region. We were there to assess the condition of the Country since the fires and to set a date for a cool burn in the national park, which was good news. Along the sandy roads we travelled once again, and all I could see was neglected land. The area where the wildfires hadn't burned was still choked up with fuel just waiting for another inferno to happen.

Across most of the land that the fires did incinerate, the trees were sick or dead. The understorey had no grass and was thick with wattles, native hops and other flammable invasive plants. We stopped in different places to talk about what we were seeing, and it was bad news for the Country. The non-Indigenous park ranger who had fought the fire with us also came along and he too shared his grief. The burn we were planning would be another attempt to try to get Aboriginal fire management into the park. It was only going to be one burn, but at least it was something for the Traditional Owners to engage in since that terrible fire.

We set off to the area where we'd done our back-burn, to see how the land had held up since that day of the so-called spot-over. When we got there, I could see that the trees were unharmed where we had back-burned and we could hear the calls of birds in the canopies. It needed another burn to take out some of the invasive natives, but otherwise it looked great. It was all smiles as we cast our eyes over the area, knowing that we'd stopped the wildfire from destroying that piece of Country.

Soon after, we travelled to where we had stopped doing the back-burn and found where the wildfire had jumped over the break. Most of the trees were dead and the thickening of invasive plants had exploded across the land. We noticed that the rainforest Country we had tried to back-burn from was untouched by the wildfire and hadn't burned at all. We had been just over a kilometre away from reaching the rainforest and that was the corridor where the wildfire had jumped. Had we been able to complete our burn, we would have made it to the rainforest and stopped that fire. Disappointment set in again as we looked at the dead trees scattered across the countryside.

Even if we had made it to the rainforest, the National Park rangers would have still back-burned 5 kilometres south of our fire line. Animals and plants had been killed, and the scorched land was so thick with invasive native hops and wattle that we found it impossible to walk through. To heal that Country will take many years and the work of applying the right fire again will be a tedious job. That is what happens when the land is treated this way. It will become even worse if we turn our backs and walk away to leave it in such a state.

Having the wildfire burn that landscape at the hot time of year has made the area even more flammable. If nothing is done to address the problem, another wildfire will come and devastate that land. It will happen again in Australia in regions where major wildfires took lives in 2009 and where, in 2020, wildfires killed billions of animals. It will happen again in Canada, America, Greece, Hawaii, Japan, Brazil – everywhere mega fires have occurred. As long as governments and authorities stay in the same old mindset we will see it happen again. I am appalled by the way fire agencies operate under their laws in Australia and in some other countries.

One time I did a burn with an Indigenous community on their traditional lands, which I will not name in respect of the times. The 200-hectare burn was in a mountainous area, and it was the first burn for that wildfire-torn region. The burn went for five days, and it took a bit of time to contain the fire due to the dry grass and rugged landscape. It was hard but the crew worked well and we managed to finish before the weekend. The next day we set off for a well-deserved break to go fishing and enjoy the countryside.

While driving past our fireground that day, I noticed a small puff of smoke on top of the escarpment. I couldn't believe it was still burning, as we'd made sure before we'd left that the fire was out and contained. Then within the next kilometre I saw a firefighting officer driving from the site. We pulled up to talk to each other through our car windows. 'Is that a fire up there?' I asked.

'Yeah, it has jumped the perimeter and got away,' he said.

I told him that I would go up and put out the fire. I had some of our crew coming behind me so there would be plenty of us to do the job.

Then the firefighter asked if I wanted any help, which made me think about it for a moment with some reluctance. Eventually I said that he could come along and lend a hand if he wanted to.

'Are you sure you want my assistance?' he asked.

'Um, if you want to come and help out then come along,' I said in a friendly way.

'So, you want me to assist, is that right?' he said again, now sounding authoritative.

'Yeah, well, come on then, let's go,' I replied, then drove off to attend the fire.

I looked into the rear-view mirror and saw that he wasn't following but had driven off in the opposite direction. That puzzled me as the invitation was clear for him to come and help out. Within the next minute or two I was at the fire and saw that it had not been burning very long at all. It must have just started when I saw that first little puff of smoke. I broke off a large branch from a tree and started to put the fire out. Then a couple of my crew turned up and worked on the other end of the fire. Within fifteen minutes we had put that fire out most of the way around and it was easy to finish off from there.

When the firefighter guy turned up, the fire was almost out but I thought it was good that he'd come along. He had a leaf blower and started controlling the last small patches of fire, but he didn't put much effort in, which I found strange. I continued to put out fires on the edges and kick burning logs into the blackened areas. It was all easy going from there and eventually we had it under control. Then the firefighter officer walked over to me.

'It looks like a hopeless case,' he said, sounding very serious.

'What do you mean? The fire is out most of the way around,' I replied. 'All we have to do now is walk around and make sure all the smoking logs are out and away from the edge.'

The firefighter didn't respond, which I found a little weird. I told him that I would go around the perimeter to finish containing the last of the fire and that was all we needed to do. When I returned there was a wall of fire right where the officer and I had stopped to talk. A drip torch was sitting over in the bush a few metres away, still burning. The fire was running in a straight line. When I hit it with the branch, flames splattered everywhere and would not go out. Seeing the flames act that way, I could tell that it was a line of fire lit by fossil fuel.

At that moment a firefighting crew turned up and the officer said his team would take it from there. They ordered us out of the fireground and announced that it was now their fire to deal with. I later learned that they receive extra hazard pay and overtime when they are out fighting a fire. They wanted to assist us with the fire to get paid, and who could blame them when the system is set up that way? Offering extra money will get more boots on the ground faster to attend to wildfire events. This is all well and good, but it is a system that pays well to respond to devastation.

I have heard a few stories from firefighting friends who have seen certain individuals allowing wildfires to linger so they would be paid more. Making money in these situations is done at the expense of the community and the environment. It is even more disturbing when it is done in the name of keeping people safe and preventing the loss of property. Wouldn't it be amazing if there was a way to pay firefighters more if they put the fire out more quickly? It would be even better if people were paid full time to go out and look after the Country all year round.

A government system that builds on environmental debt through reactiveness alone does not shine a positive light on the wildfire situation. Some old-school firefighters have told me that the industry has changed a lot since they devoted themselves to the service. That it is not the same as the days when they would go out to fight a fire simply to put it out. The question is, will it get better or will it grow worse with all this bureaucracy and corruption in the world? It needs to be addressed if fighting wildfires is going to improve into the future. I am sure there are enough good people in the agencies who will try to make that happen.

Making the land as healthy as possible is the answer to limiting the effects of wildfire and saving more lives, property and nature. If the land has constant stewardship, there will be major improvements, even if they begin on a small scale. They won't happen overnight, but they will over time if we get on with the job now. Making the land healthy by bringing back its identity needs to happen around the world. That proactive thinking creates the best form of resilience, and it is totally absent from Western management strategies.

A healthy Country will make it safer and easier to fight wildfires and create greater options for conducting back-burning. At present, firefighters are dealing with wildfires fuelled by sick landscapes clogged up with dangerous, thick woody understoreys of all sorts of weeds. Maintaining the identity of the Country through traditional management should eventually mean that fire management transitions away from the concept of hazard reduction burns. At present, firefighters are not land managers, and they should not be lighting fires unless they have experience of the land. If they did have these skills, there would already be effective programs operating across the world.

Western ways of doing things certainly aren't working, but authorities continue their practices without being held to account. Meanwhile, the land and many people and animals continue to suffer. The more we ignore the proactive approach of working with the land, the less able we will be to reduce the effects of wildfires in the future.

CHAPTER 3

Camp burn

'Camp burn' is the term my mentors used for cultural fire practised around houses and towns, or to protect traditional dwellings in the old times.

On some occasions I have had the opportunity to do camp burns around properties and landscapes prior to the wider area being affected by wildfires. In places where Aboriginal burning was done a year earlier, the towns held up well against some of the worst wildfires. Houses were saved and areas of bushland avoided incineration.

There was one property where traditional burns were carried out as a training exercise. Following devastating wildfires that came a couple of months later, that house was the only one left standing. I hoped the media would grab hold of the story about cultural burning being used to save places from the wildfires. I hoped it would lead to using camp burns on a larger scale to protect communities and towns, and that it would be an opportunity to create jobs and train cultural fire practitioners to implement camp burns around urban developed areas. So, after the wildfires of 2019–2020, I was pleased when many councils got in touch with us to instigate the use of cultural burning. With the loss of so much life and property, they were keen to use Indigenous fire programs in their towns. The art of reading Country and burning ecosystems through the Indigenous seasons are just as important for populated areas as in remote regions. The traditional practice makes the burns much safer and promotes the surrounding countryside to become beautiful and healthy. Too often I have seen hazard reduction burns near towns that leave behind scorched tree canopies and damaged soils.

Burning at the wrong time around towns makes the fire hotter and more frightening for the residents. Burns that don't follow traditional practices also encourage exotic weeds and invasive natives to return, which makes the area even more dangerously flammable. This puts the community in a vulnerable position as the landscape is open to the threat of wildfire.

Doing camp burns requires burning diverse ecosystems in the area at different times of the year with a low, cool fire. The townspeople will see multiple burns happening around their area, over a longer burning window, but they will be smaller and far gentler fires than what the residents are used to. These burns will eventually treat the entire region over the annual seasons, instead of burning it all in one go within a short time. Once the land has been carefully assessed, each camp burn creates a mosaic pattern around the town, made up of small burned areas that are black and patches that are still green, which were not burned.

The contrast of black and green (shown here as a light grey) from a cultural fire in New South Wales, demonstrating the benefits of mosaic burns.
Photo by Victor Steffensen.

Cool burns encourage renewed plant growth, so the land becomes greener and creates food for birds and animals. People will also feel more comfortable in the summer knowing that they are surrounded by healthy, resilient Country. If wildfires do come to the surrounding area, the cool burns will reduce the risk of residents having to be evacuated and the town's community can feel safe.

One time I was involved in a camp burn in a small mining town in Central Queensland, working with the Traditional Owners. It was a big block of scrubby land that was surrounded by houses, roads and the local school. This was the first contract burn for the Indigenous rangers I was training and the fuel load was through the roof. Thick guinea grass choked up most of the block, which made the fuel loads scary to burn. People who don't have the necessary knowledge or experience might be nervous to light such hazards and for that reason it rarely gets done. This only increases the risk and creates a dangerous ticking time bomb for the town.

We did the burn after a period of heavy rain to make it less stressful for the trees and to protect the soil. It was the best outcome possible and would make the town more resilient in the coming summer. As we were working, a town resident came walking by and stopped to talk to our fire crew. She told us that she used to play on the land when she was a child. It was the first time she had been able to walk through the area since then, and this time she was doing it with her three kids. She could walk in the beautiful bushland again instead of staying in her house surrounded by inaccessible undergrowth.

On another occasion I was burning bushland with an Indigenous community that lived in a busy residential area close to a major city. The land was overgrown with invasive trees and the sandy ground was full of thick leaf litter. We picked the date to do the first burn and put in one ignition point to let the fire slowly trickle its way across the area. The gums and stringy bark trees were tall and the smoke misted up through the tree canopies. It was beautiful inside the forest watching the fire. Then, with only a few steps, I walked out of the forest and on to the street lined with residential houses. We had a rural fire service fella with us for support and to show people that it was a controlled burn.

The next minute a woman started screaming out her window, 'There's a fire. Fire!' Her voice was loud and distressed, and some of the crew freaked out. We went over to see if she was okay and she soon calmed down. Other residents were looking from their front yards to see what was happening. Most of them seemed concerned but in the end, it settled into a beautiful burn. We did a second burn there the following year, which was even better than the first. By the third burn the residents were coming over and talking to us and that made it very enjoyable. They had big smiles on their faces and were appreciative of the service we were providing.

One lady brought her two children over to say hello, so I gave them a tour of the burned area to teach them why the fire was good for the land. They loved learning all that knowledge and seeing the excitement of a gentle fire just outside their front door. Every time I have burned around towns, the people have come out of their houses to have a look. Most of the time they are grateful and are always interested to learn what we are doing. Sometimes we organise a barbeque and workshop for the community and make a day of it. Managing the land around townships with cultural fire can only improve the residents' social and mental wellbeing. Introducing the full benefits of Aboriginal fire management helps to create a positive fire culture. That's why it needs to involve the whole community, so they can experience those benefits and support the practice into the future.

By contrast, having fire management practices institutionalised by government agencies excludes the public and stops them from experiencing the positive outcomes of a fearless fire culture. We have a society now that does not know what fire is or that it can be a tool in land management, and – understandably – many people are fearful of the loss of life and property they think it could bring.

We are trying to move away from the fear of traditional fire culture, and camp burns can be a major player in changing that mindset. It is inevitable that the broader population in Australia and elsewhere will have to live more closely with fire and that's why it helps to see it as a friend. I met a family in Victoria who were terrified of fire because of the infernos that had destroyed their town some years ago. The young boy of the family told me that his neighbour had died in the fires, and he has to live with that memory every day. I was horrified by this story and it made me feel for the lovely family who were innocent bystanders and not responsible for their surroundings.

I invited them to come out on Country with me and we did a little burn on my friends' property. After an hour of showing them signs in the land and explaining the nature of a good fire, I lit a small patch of grass. The boy started to cry out in fear and hid behind his father, holding onto him tightly. We comforted the little one until he quietened down and eventually the family began to relax. They were amazed by how calm the fire was and seeing this burn helped them to heal from the trauma they had endured. Usually, they would get counselling to help them with the hardship. Learning about the land and the cool fire was proving to be good medicine for them too.

One of the biggest factors to consider when burning around townships is the smoke from the fire. Often, complaints about smoke can be serious, as some people have health conditions, although some residents will complain because the smoke made their curtains smell. They may be complaining now but if the burn is not done, they might not have a house at all in the event of a catastrophic fire. That is why people need to be educated to be supportive of managing the land around their towns with fire. If you live in a fire-prone environment, you will need to learn to live with fire.

There is a greater chance of people complaining about the smoke if the fire is done the wrong way. The effects of smoke can be significantly reduced by using small, multiple burns done in the right order for healing the various ecosystems. This creates less smoke than one large burn held at the wrong time. The first burns in long-unmanaged landscapes are always the smokiest due to old fuel loads and thick vegetation. But if camp burns are done regularly and in the right season, the vegetation will become healthier and less smoky over time. The aim is to burn in a way that brings back the native grass and improves the original vegetation.

Grass fires encourage white smoke, which is gentler than toxic black smoke from weeds, a woody understorey or dead leaf litter. That is why burning for the environment is so important, not only to encourage less flammable vegetation but also to have better smoke quality. The right frequency of fire will ensure it is cool and promotes the growth of native grass. Having native grass will make it possible to burn effectively and means the burning window will be open through the cooler times of the year. Also, encouraging native grass to grow back will keep the land green and resilient throughout the drier seasons.

From long before colonisation, burning the native grass has been the main aim of cultural burning. Every time the grass becomes old and dry, the grass must burn, and in the old times it was only the grass that used to be burned. This practice encourages the growth of what we call 'second grass', which are the new shoots that come up straight after the burn. The second grass grows back a little shorter than the first grass. It stays greener longer than the first grass too, because it does not need as much moisture and the black ash from the fire gives the new grass more nutrients. The second grass keeps the soils healthy and provides food for the animals throughout the seasons. By summer the land is beautiful, clean and green and is far more resilient to any wildfires.

This knowledge is not understood today. Instead, the entire land is covered with brown grass that surrounds both bushlands and urban areas. The first grass is left lying there for years, and it does neither the environment nor urban areas any favours. Instead, it promotes wildfires and leads to less biodiversity. The land is not supposed to be brown in summer; it is meant to be green in most places and that is why we regularly burn the grass. Even in drought times, the grass can be regularly burned in the winter months, and it becomes even easier if the land has been managed properly before any unprecedented dry periods begin.

We want to get trials of long-term cultural burn programs happening to show the benefits of fire in action on a large scale. This would involve employing a trained fire crew full-time to do the work, including using harvesting techniques (which I discuss in chapters 5 and 6). Harvesting trees and the removal of invasive plants work hand in hand with cultural fire programs to care for the surrounding landscapes. It is important to document the statistics of a town becoming safer from wildfire, with less property damage due to a program of traditional burns. Then these positive outcomes should encourage more towns to implement the same strategies, creating a foundation for resilient communities. The hope is for insurance companies to become involved, to show how a town can reduce the damaging effects of wildfires and to insure the cultural fire teams. Also, if a town has an effective, ongoing camp burn program, then maybe home insurance fees in the region will become more affordable.

Even before the recent wildfires, Indigenous fire crews have always struggled to get insurance to cover them and it is only becoming harder. This is unfair because the Indigenous rangers and fire practitioners who are working to look after the land and towns need to be insured, just as government fire services are. We are trying to bring down the risk for the insurance companies, yet they won't insure Indigenous fire management teams. Do they prefer to pay out billions in property damage from wildfires instead? It really does not make any sense. It is the same for property owners who are trying to insure their houses while premiums go through the roof. In some places around the world, insurance companies are refusing cover due to the frequency of wildfires. We have to do more to look after our communities and we can do this through education around Indigenous land management.

In my work as an Indigenous fire practitioner, I have conducted many camp burns in different places, and I have seen that the land is always greener and more resilient during summer fire seasons following our program of these burns. Most of the camp burns I've done have been around Indigenous communities because the positive fire culture is already there. Not to mention that there is usually far less red tape and fewer Western authorities to deal with.

It was good to be a part of the team running a camp burn around the small village of the Yunesit'in, a First Nations community in Canada. After wildfires devastated their lands, they began work to bring their homelands back to health. I visited the school there twice with the local Indigenous fire practitioners to teach the children about good fires. During each visit, we'd sing together and I would read my children's books to them and then take them for a walk in the forest nearby to share traditional knowledge. They loved learning about the good fire – and that is the way it should be. Having children see their community caring for the land with fire is better than experiencing fearful wildfires. It is vital to connect them with cultural fire and encourage them to look up to the practitioners who are caring for the land. Nurturing a healthy fire culture that educates the community socially and environmentally will lead to keeping people safe and help us all to align ourselves with nature.

Here is a scene I hope will happen one day: A little old lady walks out of her front door to go down to the local store to do some shopping. She sees gentle white smoke over in the nearby stringybark Country and notices fire practitioners walking with the cool fire. She reminds herself that it is almost spring and the custodians of the land are finishing up their last burns for the year. There is no need to worry about the fire or to ring the emergency services in a panic. The fire practitioners are following their usual routine to keep the community safe. She knows this because her grandson tells her about it from what he has learned at school. The community has grown to live confidently with fire and has developed a greater love for the natural landscapes that surround them. It's nearly summer and the weather is dry, but the countryside is vibrant with shades of green covering the hills. There is no need to prepare, there is no cause for fear, the land is our community and the lady knows that everyone is safe.

CHAPTER 4

Memory

There is something that is magically special about memory, and the more I acknowledge it the more beautiful it becomes. Memory usually portrays the good and bad times a person has had and shared in their lifetime. If we look at the extensive memory that humanity has shared with the planet, it goes far deeper.

Memory is installed within all of creation. One perspective on memory is how it can physically present itself through Mother Nature. Indigenous practices are entrenched in the memory of the landscape due to thousands of years of stewardship. It is an evolutionary relationship between people and nature that many life forms rely on. Country remembers humanity's footprint, what we have done in the past and what we are doing today. Mother Nature is communicating with us all the time. She talks to us constantly, trying to remind us of our relationship with and responsibilities to the natural world.

Now that we are no longer applying the ancient methods of traditional fire, Western societies have limited respect for land and waters. Humanity has broken the pattern of culturally aligning with nature and, as a result, we are starting to see the decline of our natural world. It is a clear cry from Mother Nature that we have lost the memory of our very own existence. This is evident through indicators such as severe weather patterns, plant and animal extinction, poor water quality, wildfires, damaged soils and other signs that communicate her struggles.

These indicators are not new. It's just that our collective world does not take them seriously enough to react before they escalate. We should become familiar with the positive indicators that will give us a deeper connection with the land. For many people, experiencing this connection feels good because it reminds us that we are a part of nature.

The positive indicators – that is, signs of a healthy Country and a healthy planet – are expressed in the behavioural patterns of our natural world. If we align ourselves with these patterns, magic can happen. That magic is the ability to work with Mother Nature to encourage regeneration with minimal stress. The practice of applying cultural fire on the land has been doing this for so long that the plants and animals have come to depend on it. The animals know that cool fire will produce food sources that they rely on. The fresh growth of vegetation and the preservation of trees provide healthy habitats for them. Finding ways to get the right temperature in the soils will promote the growth of native plants that are local to those ecosystems. Applying old fire regimes the way the land remembers them – including during the right season and in the right place – will create a healing response from Country.

Memories are installed in the land through Indigenous practices, passed down through the generations. There are memories of people walking through the land applying fire for food, tending to the land from place to place. The skill of knowing where to apply fire showed great care by protecting Mother Nature and helping her to thrive. The only sounds were the cool fire crackling away at the native grasses, and the breeze rustling the leaves as it flowed through the trees, gently pushing the fire along to natural firebreaks. The birds chirping as the flames revealed treasures of grass seeds and insects, and the light thumping of kangaroos as they took a short hop towards a fire-resilient ecosystem to safety.

The familiar sound of people walking barefoot through the bush is what Mother Nature remembers. The courtesy of singing out to Country to let everything know that the fire is coming. The chatter of ancient language between countrymen and women ricocheting through the trees. The people were recognisable to the area through their appearance and smell, and they blended into the natural landscape. The only tools they held as they lit up the grass were a set of firesticks and some burning bark. Their Country was left with a mosaic of black and green as the plants continued to thrive under a lush, healthy canopy.

There is the memory of minimal stress because the fire was applied in a way that the land expected, which has formed the Indigenous fire culture over generations. Every indicator to where the flames go out, what the fire doesn't burn, the gentle white smoke, the gestures of the animals all entwined into expressing what was good for the land and how people were a vital part of that kinship. This is what the land experienced for so long, what the land remembered until the ancient custodianship of Country was interrupted. As it would with any part of nature, the disruption caused a breakdown in the collective lifecycle. This stark change to humans' relationship with Country has caused so much pain in the natural world.

Nature's relationship with humans has now been diverted into an environmental breakdown. Mother Nature is a victim of destructive human behaviour, which has become her recent memory. The modern ways of applying fire are far from being aligned with the memory of the landscape. Modern firefighters pick an area that they see as a threat, or ecologists may pick a fire zone based on the recommendations of Western science. Their fire crews arrive on Country with a convoy of trucks carrying a range of machinery, to undertake what seems like a military operation. Helicopters are on standby, while flashing red and blue lights flicker to the piercing beeping sounds of trucks reversing. The bulldozer starts up and begins to push its way through the bush to make a bare dirt firebreak. Knocking over trees, leaving their roots sticking up in the air, creating a scar on the land that will take a long time to heal. Mechanical land clearing becomes a bizarre form of fire management that the natural world has never experienced before.

The loud sounds of water pumps begin to echo across the landscape as the fire trucks prepare for the prescribed blaze to start. Firefighters light their drip torches filled with fossil fuels, ready to pour the fuel over the land. Without warning, they walk a line of petroleum-fed fire along the edge of their burn zone. The noise of leaf blowers adds to the rumbling choir of engines, as they fan the fire to control it to their liking. There are no natural sounds to be heard, drowned out by the machinery required by Western practices. The Country is in shock from the intrusion of fire crews persistently applying new methods with no alignment to what the land remembers.

When the land experiences the impact of these unfamiliar ways, the response is rarely a positive one. I have seen so many landscapes treated this way and it often leaves the area lifeless and empty. In most cases you can hear a pin drop; not a sound can be heard, just a sickly silence. Sometimes the land looks like a war zone, where every tree standing is scorched in baked soils. It takes a long time for Country to recover from the shock. When this treatment becomes repetitive it turns into torture for the land. This leads to a slow degeneration that eventually causes chronic illness and results in the decline of flora and fauna.

For most Aboriginal people, it is hard to take part in the Western ways of applying fire because these ways do not feel right within their spirit. Although some Indigenous people may have lost much knowledge of the land, there is still a strong connection to their Country through the memory of their Ancestors. That uncomfortable feeling is usually a gut reaction that comes from our intuition. I have been told many stories from Indigenous people who have taken part in Western burns and then quit their jobs because of these uneasy feelings. It is no different to watching someone abusing another human; it is unquestionably wrong. We know too well that traumatic events cause bad memories for the land as well as for humans. Continuous mistreatment can affect people physically and mentally, leading to, for example, sickness, starvation, stress and even death. We are no different from Mother Nature. That's why the Old People would talk to the land and respectfully treat Country just like a person. These days, modern society takes the world for granted, and some foolishly believe that the world was created for their own disposal.

Plants hold an abundance of memories linked to people, through traditional food and medicinal use. I remember walking with one of my mentors through the bush, hunting for wild pigs, when we stumbled across a blackcurrant bush loaded with fruit. We were happy to find these berries because they are tasty and sweet, despite being so tiny. I started to pick them one by one, which was a very slow process that took a bit of concentration. The Old Man walked up to the shrub and simply snapped off a branch that was covered in fruit.

'See here, this is how the Old People used to pick the fruit from this bush,' he said, as he snapped off another branch to demonstrate. 'They break the branch off and take it back to camp with all the fruit still on. Then they sit down with a branch each and have a good feed.' The Old Man then held the branch above his head and began nibbling the berries as if he were feasting on a bunch of grapes.

It made perfect sense to me, while picking the fruit one by one didn't feel like the right way to do it. I reached out and broke a branch for myself and noticed that it snapped off without any effort at all. I could snap the branches between two fingers and it felt incredibly good to do so. The Elder went on to tell me that pruning the branches this way made the fruit trees short and bushy. This encouraged a good crop of fruit for the next season.

As I broke off a few more I could feel that the plant loved having its branches removed. The fact that they grew back healthier and more plentiful was a clear indicator of this too. I've tried this pruning technique with other fruit trees that were traditionally harvested this way and found that all their branches snapped off just as easily. Out west in the red sand Country of Australia, some Elders showed me the shrub they used for making windbreaks. They snapped off the tall, woody branches with their bare hands and then used them to make a wall to sit behind to hide from the cold wind. By the look of the thick, woody stems, I guessed that it was a very tough plant. But to my amazement, each branch snapped off with ease. It was a beautiful example of human and animal actions instilled into the memory of these plants.

It seemed more than a coincidence that the branches of many similar plants snapped off easily. After countless generations harvesting plants this way, it was as if they had evolved by allowing their branches to be brittle. Breaking off branches from plants that were not traditionally harvested this way resulted in the opposite response. With one plant, I had to twist and twist the branch to break it off, as the fibres would not let go. I found that many plants whose branches would not break were more poisonous or, to my knowledge, didn't have uses that required their branches to be removed. These plants were used by taking the bark, root, timber or leaves to produce the special gifts they had to offer.

Observing the physical memory indicators in these plants and how they were used in the past helped me to understand the traditional knowledge processes even more. It is so beautiful to feel for Country, and in turn that it remembers the ancient connections of human relationship. The way nature responds positively to ancient practices is a recording of a time when we were in tune with the natural world.

As individuals, it is devastating to forget moments of our lives and eventually forget who our loved ones are. We know this from the experiences of people with memory-loss diseases such as Alzheimer's. We also have a collective condition of memory loss that is detrimental to our natural world. Many societies have forgotten who they are as humans, along with their cultural identities and relationship with the planet. Losing our collective human memory results in the loss of principles, values, knowledge and practice. We become oblivious to the solutions humans have known before and what should naturally come from our instinct.

Among the memories we have in our minds today are those of recent human histories of colonisation and wars. These events can erase long-term human memories stored in cultures and ways of life that have existed within the natural world for millennia. Mother Nature can create a massive flood across the landscape to show people that you should not build houses there, ever. But modern policies will give approval to build there if the area has not flooded in 50 to 100 years. The 2025 floods of the Guadalupe River in Kerr County, Texas, in the United States, created a tragic outcome that cannot be forgotten. Yet this is a well-known flood plain with a history of devasting flood loss. The massive 2020 wildfires in Australia have already been forgotten by many, which means that nothing is being done to avoid the same catastrophe happening again.

People today endure major floods, wildfires, droughts and pandemics as if they had never occurred before. Do they not know that these natural events have already happened long before the recorded memory of modern society? Flood plains have evolved over thousands of years, and just because these places haven't flooded in the last 200 years, it doesn't mean they won't eventually. Flood plains and catchments are a recording of nature's history. They are signs that the land will flood again, only next time there will be towns in the way. Just like someone with memory loss, the people, governments and organisations will think it's never happened before. So often, society has a collective short memory of nature and her previous relationships with humanity, so the same mistakes are made over again. Events that occur today are often forgotten tomorrow, just as the towns on flood plains are rebuilt in exactly the same place.

If we forget our deep memories with the land, then we lose our way as a people and the land loses the practices that it relies on. The rock art sites all over the world remind us that we must never forget how the natural world remembers us. The paintings depicted on the cave walls remind us that our Ancestors across the globe lived with the land, as opposed to the way so many people ignore Mother Nature now. Reinstating traditional knowledge practices is a pathway to opening the mind, to bringing back the collective memory within nature and ourselves.

Recovering traditional practices to address modern solutions will quickly get things on track again. This can be done through stories, paintings, books, songs and ultimately within our governance, just like Indigenous cultures have done for millennia. Aligning ourselves with the memory of the land and seas can bring healing to the planet, supporting the knowledge of our Ancestors to ensure we do not become a bad memory for Mother Nature ever again.

CHAPTER 5

Harvesting for solutions

One of my favourite things is to walk on Country with the Old People and learn about the traditional uses of plants – from the grasses to small plants and shrubs, leading up high into the big, old parent trees. Every plant has its own character and special gifts that it has shared with our Ancestors since the Dreaming. The best parts of these walks are preparing the medicines, harvesting the fruits and making artefacts.

Most people are aware of some of the traditional uses for plants, but may think little of the importance of harvesting them. Plants love to be harvested and that's why they are here, along with taking care of all elements of Country. Harvesting can help plants grow stronger and it keeps their ecosystems healthy and plentiful, if done in the right way. It is another important form of Indigenous stewardship and a valuable practice that is not well understood today.

The First Peoples around the world used the land's natural resources all the time, unlike today when the vegetation is sadly left lonely and neglected, gathering large deposits of litter build-up in many places. It is like a house that nobody lives in anymore; the people who once tended to these plants have gone. Animals also had harvesting techniques that kept plants stimulated to help them thrive. With the gradual decline of native animals, they are also missed by the plants. Some plants will not grow unless they are eaten and their seeds deposited across the land through specific animal droppings.

The cabbage palm in Australia is a good example of an ancient tree that was made for harvesting. People used the young suckers (the new shoots) for food and the new inner leaves were harvested regularly for weaving, which all helped to stop the plants from overpopulating. Their large flat leaves made great plates and were also used as a housing material; this always left the palms pruned to a tidy state. The sandy ground in which they grew was clean from people walking around them, and the leaves did not get the chance to die off to create a heavy build-up of litter. Today, the cabbage palm and similar plants are often choked up with years of dead leaves just waiting for a fire to engulf them.

Cabbage palms don't like fire. If they do burn it takes them a long time to recover and sometimes they do not survive at all. Even plants that do like fire are badly affected by intense heat from too many dead leaves and bark burning around their roots. Fire practitioners need to rake the dead leaves and fronds away from the base of plants such as cabbage and coconut palms before burning. The preferred solution is to cut off the green leaves when they are plentiful and use them, rather than just removing dead waste later. This level of land management will create broader benefits to the environment and community.

As I wrote in the previous chapter, snapping branches off some fruit trees can increase their harvest. There have been countless times when I have stood with others looking at native fruit trees and noticing a poor crop. Some say that this is due to climate change. No doubt climate is a factor in certain cases, but it can also be because the tree is no longer harvested by people or animals. These days, many fruit trees grow to be tall and stringy instead of short and bushy. If the surrounding parent tree population is too dense that can also affect the fruiting capacity and growth of the tree.

Just as my mentor taught me, I show fire practitioners how to snap off the branches of particular trees when the fruiting season is over. Even if people don't eat the fruit, this process helps improve the food source for birds and other animals. There are many interrelationships in the natural world, which is why Indigenous plant knowledge is so extensive. But it must come with knowing the right time and method to harvest according to the Indigenous seasonal calendar. Restoring harvesting knowledge will teach us a lot about how we can better care for the land into the future. These practices can also connect us to nature.

Fire practitioners need to learn this cultural harvesting knowledge and make it part of their duties. It goes hand in hand with fire knowledge. Practising fire management and harvesting can create important full-time work all year round. Linking these practices together will allow more land to be cared for and stimulated at the same time. That is how it was before, and rebuilding this relationship is essential if people are going to effectively manage and restore biodiversity on the planet.

People often talk about harvesting grains and about Australian Aboriginal people being the first bread makers, but the knowledge goes far deeper than that. By no means can it be called 'agriculture' in the sense of colonised farming practices. That is the wrong word to describe the native harvesting practices of Indigenous peoples. There have been debates in Australia over declaring that Aboriginal people were the first agriculturalists. The truth is that the Old People did not alter the land to grow crops, as happens with modern farming practices. They harvested the land in ways that kept it undisturbed, so it retained its natural state.

The only word in the English language I can think of that describes the sustainable way Aboriginal people harvested the land is 'gardening'. That is because people were tending to the land and taking from plants in a way that also took care of them. It is a far more beautiful word than 'agriculture' because gardening has love entrenched within the practice. It's like when people say their plants grow better when they talk to them and apply a little love. In the case of the Indigenous application, gardening is bound by traditional lore to ensure the practice happens and the love is entrenched within spirituality.

Indigenous plant use is a highly respectful interaction, creating activation and stimulation that fulfills people's needs while helping nature to thrive. It's a clear example of praction, a word that comes from a story I wrote in *Fire Country*. 'Praction' means applying a human action to the land that benefits everything in nature while we receive what we need in return. There is much to learn from that statement; it underpins sustainable methods that we rarely see in practice today.

Modern cattle farmers recognise the benefits of not overworking the land and allowing it to rest from livestock, which is known as cell grazing. Our Ancestors understood that giving the land a rest is crucial to any practice of extracting needs from the Earth. That is why the nomadic lifestyle linked to Indigenous people was a beautiful symbiotic process that helped to maintain a respectful balance for the land. There is so much to learn from traditional knowledge that can help improve modern landcare practices. These practices, including fire management, may be the seeding ground for many mainstream solutions. The land has all the answers and they are right under our noses in the simplest of forms.

A few years ago, I went back to my mother's Country for our Tagalaka people's celebration of the tenth anniversary of our native title. It had been ten years since the government legally recognised the land as being Tagalaka Country before and since colonisation. As I crossed the Gilbert River in North Queensland and ventured into our vast traditional homelands, I could see nothing but lancewood and golden wattle trees everywhere. While these trees are native to other parts of our Country, they are not supposed to be growing in the landscape I was driving through. Up there, they were creating a monoculture, contributing greatly to the loss of biodiversity. The colonial practices of timber-cutting, grazing of livestock and incorrect fire regimes had stimulated this problem for decades

Wherever invasive plants such as lancewood or wattles dominate, they tend to kill the native grasses by dropping their acidic leaves onto the ground. Killing off the ground vegetation native to that place will make the invasive species more resilient. Many invasive native plant species come from no-fire Country; they are fire sensitive and their traditional ecosystems are managed by not burning them. But when they take over fire-dependent ecosystems where the local parent trees coexist with native grasses, they contribute to a long process of extinction. Tagalaka Country has very few native grasses in the affected areas because of these invasive plants, and less grass means fewer animals. This is causing a major breakdown through the loss of identity for many different landscapes, and it is a problem that people need to fix.

Driving through the region, it broke my heart to see the slow death creeping across the land. In their rightful place, lancewood trees are very useful; their ecosystem is like a hardware store for our Country. The timber is as hard as steel and it's impossible to break a solid stick of lancewood with human strength alone. The wood was used to make digging sticks, clapsticks and fighting sticks, and the young long, thin trees were used to makes fighting spears. The roots of the lancewood tree are shallow and shoot out long, sharp shards horizontally under the surface of the ground. The timber is so poisonous that one splinter is known to have caused major health issues. Even the dead timber is dangerous and has killed horses when they have scratched their legs on dead roots sticking out of the ground. It is difficult to burn lancewood timber because of its steel-like strength, and usually even after the fire has gone out, the wood is still sitting there in its solid form.

I love the tree when it grows in its place of origin, but it becomes a major issue when it is a native invasive. The cattle farmers

I have spoken to about the invasive lancewood problem say the land is now useless and no longer supports a productive livelihood. They will usually turn their backs on it and see it as a problem that is too big or complex to fix.

It was at this stage in my drive through my mother's Country that I thought how good it would be to test the lancewood in science labs, to see if it could be used for something. If that were possible, then we could harvest it from the land where it didn't belong and hopefully create a sustainable business for my community. There are thousands of hectares of the troublesome plant and we wouldn't run out of supply. After that trip I couldn't get the lancewood out of my head, which led me to thinking about other invasive plants that are contributing to extinction problems across Australia.

What many people see as a sick, lifeless landscape might be the total opposite if we were to look at it another way. Regardless of whether the lancewood could be used for anything or not, the land had to be healed. Removing the trees with fire was one way, but the lancewood trees were so tall that they were less likely to be affected by the heat of cool burning alone. On top of that, the land would then be covered with hard dead timber that would entangle the vegetation on the ground for years to come, suppressing the native grasses and plants. It is important to completely remove any vegetation that does not originally come from the ecosystem where it is growing. If a plant does not belong there when it is alive, then it should not remain there when it is dead.

When a eucalyptus tree dies in its own Country, it will usually stand dead for a long time. It will continue to serve a purpose for its ecosystem as a habitat for animals, who can live in its hollowed-out trunk and branches. Orchids can still grow on it, and the tree continues to hold the soils and give nutrients to the micro-organisms. We never cut down the dead parent trees when we use harvesting techniques. When the parent tree eventually falls, it does so with great force and indents itself in the ground. Animals, such as the echidna, crawl into the hollow trunk for shelter and feed on the insects that are running around inside it. Under the fallen log, ants, spiders, snakes and all kinds of creepy crawlies live between the soil and the heavy wood. This creates a safe place when burning, as the log habitat does not burn when we are burning the right vegetation types with good timing. Eventually, the old log will start to rot and fine sawdust will appear; that is the sign that it is finally ready to burn away into a fine ash. The lifecycle of the parent tree – from a seedling to an Elder and then to rest peacefully on its Country – is such a beautiful thing.

When the lancewood and most other invasive plants die in foreign lands, the process usually plays out the opposite way. After the lancewood has contributed to the decline of the native vegetation in its living form, it continues to cause problems when it is dead. When stringy trees like this die and fall to the ground, they do not hit the soil hard like the large parent trees. Instead, their light stringy dead bodies sit just above the ground, leaving space under their trunks. This does not create any habitat for the underground creatures, but it does take up lots of space that further suppresses the native vegetation. The thin trunks of these invasive natives do not hollow out, so they don't turn into habitats for any animals either.

In many landscapes where this type of overpopulation occurs, the ground is littered with dead trees, choking the Country. This also happens after a wildfire; it kills the trees but promotes invasives to shoot back more thickly. Harvesting and removing the invasive trees from the land will ensure that they do not burn in a cool fire. Leaving them to burn will create a hotter fire and produce the wrong temperatures in the soils, which promotes the wrong seed bank to thrive. Burning them also produces the wrong type of ash; it affects the soil and slows the regrowth of native plants.

There are also situations that involve the overpopulation of young parent trees in their traditional landscapes. When the land loses its identity this way it can be brought back to good health, but that takes lots of hard work. It is work that younger generations could be encouraged to do, and in the process they will learn so much from the land and the way it responds to their care. Creating jobs is what it is all about – supporting cultural employment strategies that will lead to meaningful work. Investing in people and Country at the same time is a big step towards re-aligning people with Mother Nature.

No doubt we will hear the same old complaints from the sceptics, who will ask, 'How are we meant to pay for it all and why?' But if the process can contribute to restoring biodiversity, reducing the risk of wildfire, improving agriculture and creating new industries then maybe it can be a good investment. Maybe harvesting can contribute, as a means of financial support, to address the problems that spiral from degraded landscapes. If we are smart, we can connect more deeply with Mother Nature to find the answers to even the most difficult questions.

While standing on my mother's Country looking at the invasives suppressing the land, it suddenly dawned on me: maybe nature was trying to tell us something by creating this sea of menacing invasive natives. But maybe there was something a little more positive that the land was trying to tell us. Maybe the land was saying, 'Hey, stop cutting down the old trees and treating me the way you have been treating me for the last 200 years. Instead of cutting down the old trees, take what I have produced for you in tenfold and use that to make what you need.'

Those words that came from Tagalaka Country were echoing in my head as I cast my eyes across the devastated parts of the landscape. Then the words from the cattlemen I had heard earlier came to mind, about the land being useless now. Maybe I was looking at a sea of lancewood that could be harvested to make products that could replace logging native forest, digging the minerals out of the earth, polluting our air, or sucking up the fresh water from our rivers. Mother Nature still provides us with a solution, even when the problem has been caused by our own actions.

Not long after that day on Country, my thoughts must have been heard by the universe as we were invited to connect with a science lab at a university. They were making amazing products out of all sorts of material wastes, including outdated computers and broken glass. Receiving the invitation was exciting as I've always wanted to work with Western science labs to support traditional knowledge innovation. After a couple of online meetings, I visited the university and met their clever team in person. They were a happy group of scientists who were passionate about the work they were doing to help the planet.

What they created from old appliances that would otherwise have gone into landfill was mind blowing. They showed me objects they'd made from old Covid face masks and from fishing nets collected from beaches where they had been washed up. Then they presented me with a tile made from a sample of wood. It was beautiful to hold and was very cool and modern.

I explained the techniques of Indigenous harvesting and the massive problem of invasive plants destroying so much Country. After that, a proposal was submitted. We all knew, though, that getting the project approved and underway would be a long process. There is so much bureaucracy involved in protecting intellectual property and so much red tape when trying to sort out the legalities with the universities that community-led innovation becomes almost impossible. My hope is that one day we will have our own laboratories and employ scientists full time to work on the many innovative projects that can be developed with traditional knowledge. Then we can get on with what needs to be done more efficiently, without the system getting in the way. We can overcome the hurdles that for far too long have stopped Indigenous communities from creating opportunities.

It might have been a dream to start with, but the determination was there to find a process to make it a reality. Before long, I was driving back out to Tagalaka Country to collect lancewood samples. An opportunity like this could bring greater chances to heal the land and community. The harvesting could be revolutionary in demonstrating a way to support new solutions with multiple benefits for many regions. Not having a use for the trees would make the task a lot harder, because there would less motivation if there were no business prospects attached.

The clever thing the land has done with its monoculture presentation is to create a different invasive plant for every region. Some areas have a few invasive characters to choose from. In Tasmania the Hakea plant is taking over the highlands, in parts of southern Queensland there is Cypress pine, and in other parts of Australia there are she-oak infestations. In New Mexico in the United States, there are juniper plants that suppress the land. All over the world there are invasive plants that are trying to tell us something. A different plant for every region is a different niche for every community to work on. It's as if Mother Nature gave every region something different to help share the opportunity for innovation.

At first, my hope was to establish more income streams for the regions, to create more jobs and broaden career opportunities. It may be that Indigenous knowledge can create a broad-ranging solution based on healing Country, instilling the knowledge in young people, restoring cultural identity and sparking innovative ways to reverse the harm done to our planet. What I am explaining here is just the tip of the iceberg, because there is so much that humanity still does not know about Mother Nature. One thing that's certain, there are plenty of invasive plants that are choking the land, which makes that problem a good place to start such endeavours. These projects could do farmers and private landholders a great favour by having harvesting crews fix their land and improve their livelihoods and properties. They might create a great exchange that could boost relationships and productivity in the regions based on healing Country.

The invasive vegetation problem, or thickening of the land by these monocultures, will likely be an intergenerational task

Admiring a bloodwood tree that has been freed of invasive plants on Tagalaka Country in North Queensland, Australia. Photo by Bella Liafoo.

due to the massive tracts of land that they cover. If there is still demand for the product once the invasive plants have been removed, then maybe it will be worth planting these species. It could be that we create a testing ground to find new crops for the future to replace the crops that extract too much from our Country – new crops that use very little water and no chemicals. In some cases, we could grow these plants simply by applying a hot fire across the soil. Perhaps this process is also a way to bring traditional and Western knowledge together to come up with solutions and new ideas.

More studies and trials need to be done as we are only scratching the surface in exploring these solutions. We may not have cracked the code for ways to use the lancewood or golden wattle trees yet, but we must keep trying for the sake of the affected landscapes. No matter what the research and testing leads to, we will learn so much along the way. Using traditional knowledge systems supported by clever young Western scientists might well be one of the first steps towards healing our sick planet. The testing ground for nature-based solutions can only come from Country, and we need to care for Country if we want prosperity for one and all.

CHAPTER 6

Free the trees

Trees are the ancient Elders of the land. For thousands of years they have coexisted with humans across many continents, providing countless treasures that support the gift of life on Earth. For Indigenous people, they are the vital component of living with the land for millennia. Every tree has a far greater purpose than the general roles they're known for, such as providing oxygen, conserving water, enriching the soils and supporting wildlife. The trees have so many hidden secrets and the older they grow the more powerful they become, sharing amazing wonders beyond anyone's dreams.

When learning about trees from my mentors, there was one aspect of lore that stood out for me. That rule was to never kill the big, old parent tree when taking resources from them to fulfill your needs. If you needed to use the roots of the tree, then only digging out one or two roots was the rule. Then you had to cover the dirt back over to leave the ground as it was before.

If you had to cut out a slab of wood or bark from the trunk, then you did so without ringbarking the tree (removing a ring of bark from around the trunk, which can eventually kill the tree). All over Australia today, you can find healthy trees that are hundreds of years old bearing scars from Indigenous use long before colonisation.

Keeping the tree alive means that it can continue to provide further gifts through its leaves, seeds, bark, sap, fruit, flowers, roots and wood. Most importantly, it means the tree can carry on its important role of supporting all life on Earth. When the first settlers came to Australia, they saw massive old-growth trees spread throughout the land. The areas where the trees stood were like well-tended parks, with a diversity of native grasses, herbs, fungi and small plants. Many of those smaller plants can't exist without the larger trees, as they need each other to create their ecological communities. Cutting down old-growth forests leads to a biological breakdown that causes the flora and fauna to fade away.

The Old People knew which trees would produce the maximum benefits of food and medicines and they encouraged their growth. The plant-based foods fed not only humans but also animals, and that led to diversity of life across the land. The right forest structure let the trees flourish. When the trees grew old this way, in their own ecosystems, it made the land healthier and more resilient against unprecedented changes in climate or threats of fire, floods or invasive plants. And a healthy landscape was easier for the people to manage.

The European settlers didn't see the genius of the natural forests, nor the many uses of the trees. They could only see the value of the timber, and the way to retrieve it was to chop down and kill the tree. The destruction of trees 100 years old and more cut off so many interrelated benefits of life. If the timber was not used then trees were chopped down and burned anyway, to clear the land for foreign livestock. In Australia, the settlers were told that they could keep parcels of land for farming on the condition that they cut down all the trees. Today there are landscapes that stretch forever without a tree in sight, due to this sad destruction of the native forests.

I visited a remote pastoral property that was owned by the third- and fourth-generation descendants of one of those very first pioneers. They were a beautiful family who wanted to care for the land, and they knew that their forefathers' approach to clearing it was not a good one. I travelled with them across their property and they told me that their grandparents had cut down the trees as instructed. The trees they didn't have time to cut down were ringbarked, which satisfied the government as that was also an acceptable way to clear the land. As we drove along, I sat in the back seat of the truck, looking at the massive dead trees that were still standing after so many years. All over Australia I have seen countless dead giant trees with ringbark marks, especially in the southern areas where colonisation began.

The family kept the original land ownership deeds in a safe and they showed them to me. I could not believe my eyes as I read the words about clearing the land for ownership. As the old growth was cut down, the land became drier, the soils became harder, and the water began to seep away to muddy pools; this all contributed to making the land bare and lifeless. Once the parent trees were gone, much of the diversity of plants and animals went with them. Opening up the land allowed invasive natives and introduced buffel grass – now a serious environmental threat in Australia – to take over, creating monocultures of weeds that suppressed the countryside. This dangerous vegetation fuels the wildfires that we see today. In turn, the intensifying effects of wildfires contribute to the declining health of the land, leading to greater depths of hardship.

Old-growth parent trees play an important role in maintaining their own ecosystems. They can thin out the forest themselves when they are hundreds of years old. Grandfather and grandmother trees also teach the younger trees how to grow and stop them from growing too close together. When these old trees are no longer there, the young regrowth saplings must lead the way on their own so the forest starts up all over again, and they struggle to create their own structure and spacing. They do not have the guidance of the older trees, nor do they have the strength to prevent the spread of invasive plants.

After a forest is cleared and left to start again, the young trees shoot up in uncontrollable numbers and grow very close together. Weeds and other invasive trees often take over and the landscape thickens to a mess you cannot walk through. The young trees compete with each other, their growth is stunted and they are often stringy and thin. Growing too close together, they can bang into each other in the wind and this knocks off their leaves and bark, which then smother the forest floor. Along with the lack of sunlight, the dense tree canopy makes it harder for native grasses and plants to grow.

When a forest is like this, it will be almost impossible for it to retain its true identity and it cannot support life the way it is supposed to. Instead, it builds up fuel in the form of dense vegetation and litter that generates a time bomb to set off the next mega wildfire. This is why maintaining the old-growth trees is so important: to keep the natural structure of the forest, which will allow all species of plant life to thrive.

The tree community is no different from our own communities in the modern human world. Just imagine if the millions of citizens of a major city like New York were all thirteen years old, with no other age groups of people – only thirteen-year-olds running around everywhere. It would be chaotic, as the youngsters would get out of control or find it hard to manage without adults. There would be no parents or grandparents to guide them and help them grow. Keeping tree communities in order within the natural world is the same as keeping order within our own society. Just like the tree Elders, so too are human Elders culturally important in Indigenous family traditions, because they have the wisdom and knowledge to guide the young people.

Through our ancient human history across much of the world, we share DNA with the trees. This is not only through spiritual connections, but the countless ways plants are absorbed into our bodies: eating the fruits, rubbing the oils into our skin or climbing the trees and scraping our skin on the bark. There are generations of connections between humans and plants. This means we have a role to play in helping trees restore their health, and recognising that this role is part of Indigenous cultural knowledge.

Drawing on Indigenous knowledge can help us deal with the problem of too many trees growing in one place. When a fire-dependent ecosystem is overpopulated by young trees and not enough parent trees, we should assist nature to bring back the natural structure. This is most important in fire-dependent systems that need native grass to populate their understorey. Rainforests and other no-fire Country systems don't need harvesting as much, but harvesting practices still have a purpose in these ecosystems. To explain what is meant by no-fire Country, the Old People didn't burn every ecosystem. For example, much of the wet rainforest and other related systems don't need burning to stay healthy. In fact, most rainforests and fire-sensitive ecosystems will die if they are burned, which is why we restrict fire from these areas to care for them.

When applying the harvesting techniques, we aim to remove the overcrowded young trees to give the parent trees more space. We make sure to identify the biggest trees to keep, ensuring the trees are no less than 15 to 30 metres apart. A good crew then helps to cut down the thin, smaller trees and carries them out and away from the area. We mainly cut the trees low to the ground, so when we do a cultural burn of the area later, the fire will kill off the stumps and any regrowth. It is crucial that fallen thin trees are also taken out of the system to avoid suppressing the soils and to stop them from creating extensive fuel loads to support hot fires.

Once the larger trees are freed from all the younger ones of any species crowding around them, you can stand back and admire them. The parent trees immediately look happier as they finally have room to breathe, grow and encourage the diverse ground vegetation from their community. This is how people can help speed up the process of restoring old-growth forests, rather than leaving the trees to struggle on their own. In many places where the thickening young native forest occurs, you will find the stumps of the old trees that were cut down during and after colonisation. Finding a few stumps together will give you an indication of the structure of the forest as it was and an idea of how big the trees were. This observation is quite powerful and provides information that we can use as we work to heal each forest type.

When there is more space between the trees they are able to stretch out fully until their leaves almost touch each other. That will form canopies that allow the right amount of sunlight and shade to promote the native grasses and plants to populate the forest floor. Also, when the trees are correctly spaced, it creates a canopy bridge for animals that need to cross from tree to tree. In Australia the sugar glider possum needs to be able to jump and fly from one tree to another. If the trees are too far apart, the sugar glider will fall to the ground and become easy prey for predators.

On occasions, a problematic invasive tree might be in the mix. If there are no parent trees to fill the gaps, then it is alright to leave a large invasive native tree there to play the role until the parent trees grow and take over their rightful place. Leaving some invasive plants in bare areas may also support nesting and create a refuge for animals until the native plants return. Everything needs to be considered carefully when restructuring vegetation because restoring the identity of landscapes is a slow transitional process and not a quick fix. As the trees grow, the Country works to keep the ecosystem healthy or return to good health. Drawing on cultural indicators to create the work plan will mean less equipment and stress, and more confidence to undertake the process.

In all the areas where I have been involved in harvesting the young trees, the results have been amazing. Native grasses appear, the tree canopy thickens, leaves begin to shine, animals start to show a presence again, and the people who live in the area become motivated to connect to Country. This process of freeing the trees and using harvesting techniques is crucial.

In the United States, some Native American groups have also recognised the benefits of this process of harvesting along with traditional fire management. They too are finding that restoring a forest's good health results in a greater diversity of plants and animals. Through their work they are restoring cultural landscapes just as we are doing in Australia.

Western conservation has a similar process called bush or forest regeneration. While it is a good start, many people who are involved in it do not understand the cultural relationships with the landscape's identity. I've found that it is difficult to convince Western management agencies to listen and collaborate with Indigenous people to refine the best methods to deal with fire. There are also issues when Western vegetation laws clash with Indigenous plant use and land management practices, which need to be better understood.

One time in regional Australia, I was running a workshop with community and government people in an overpopulated eucalypt forest. With so many thin young trees and the indicators of declining ground vegetation, it was a perfect time to talk about restoring identity through harvesting. I told the group about the practice of careful harvesting, using the axe in my hand to point out the trees that needed to be removed and the ones that should stay. I walked over to one good-sized tree and pointed to a bunch of thin suckers crowding around its base. I decided to use this tree as a demonstration of cutting the smaller ones growing around it. As soon as I sunk the axe into the first stringy tree, I heard a gasp and felt a sense of unease coming from the participants.

The staff from the government land management agencies looked on with mouths open and shocked faces. I then realised why they were alarmed. What I had just done was cut down a tree in a national park and it was against their laws. But once I gave a full explanation, the group began to settle down. So I went on and cut out the rest of the young trees that were crowding the larger one. I picked a couple of volunteers from the group to take the small trees off the site to complete the process. The participants got the message, but some of them came up to me at the end and said that I had broken Western land management law in a state forest.

It is a clear policy hurdle that comes from Western laws, and I see it as a double-edged sword. It's good to protect the right trees but it is devastating to protect the wrong ones. What we experienced that day in the national park was an example of Western land management not understanding Country through the Indigenous lens. Their policies are unwittingly threatening the health of the land. If we are going to assist old-growth forests to recover and restore their identity, then we need to review these policies. This can only be done through a variety of case studies.

The Living Knowledge Network is now running some research projects with Indigenous and broader communities to collect statistics that will show how the land's health will benefit from harvesting practices. Basically, the need is to validate that the traditional knowledge methods are effective and successfully do what they intend to do: bring the native grasses back, improve the trees and return the native animals from that place to Country. One aim is to demonstrate how the old knowledge is still applicable in a changed landscape, to support our current social and economic challenges. Above all, it is to show people what Country is supposed to look like from the lens of Indigenous understanding of the identity of the land.

If we can show how the land is improving through traditional harvesting practices, then maybe government policies can be changed along the way. This work can become a major part of restoring landscapes into the future as it sits alongside Aboriginal fire practices. More jobs will need to be created in many regions and it may take generations to get through it all. If communities are given the capacity to undertake this work, we will see a major shift in the health of this continent. It will certainly contribute to reducing the risk of wildfires and other disastrous natural events.

There is no time to waste. Let's create the training and the jobs and give the communities the frontline responsibility of freeing the trees. Badly affected landscapes cannot do it on their own and without help. It is time to bring the custodians back onto the land, to help restore the trees in places where 500-year-old trees once grew. We may not see trees grow huge and old in our lifetime, but our great-great-grandchildren will, and they will be grateful that we woke up just in time.

CHAPTER 7

The skin of the Earth

When you walk on Country, it is good to take notice of everything that makes up the identity of the place. From the trees to the rivers, the type of rocks, the hills, right down to the different soils that are the skin of our Earth. While many people notice the soil only vaguely, if at all, it is the essence of the land they are standing on. Whether it is sandy, topsoil, clay, stone, basalt, bauxite or mud, the soil contributes to the diversity of Country. Everything from creation comes from the ground and goes back to the soil in the end.

Within every ecosystem, the soils have their own characteristics that tell an ancient story for each place. They can tell us about the land's history, going right back to when our world was created. They can even tell us what events happened in the past and how people lived with the land a long time ago. The soils indicate the diverse communities of trees and plants that come from the ground. In Australia, sandy soils commonly support communities of bloodwoods and stringybark trees, which grow in my homeland and many others. Every native parent tree has a strong connection with the soils in its homeland.

There is a complex mix of soil characteristics that combine to support the trees. In areas of Australia where sand mixes with light greyish topsoil, you will commonly find bloodwood and eucalyptus trees growing there. At the place where the soil changes, you will see that the trees will change with it. These indicators are key to practices such as cultural burning and knowing where to camp, hunt or forage. There are also different species of native grasses that come from a range of soil types, from the thin, wiry grasses that live in sandy places to the larger plump species that live in the rich, darker soils. These are but a few indicators of applied knowledge that let us understand the identities of Country.

Every part of Mother Nature is respected and governed through cultural lores, and this includes the earth under our feet. For example, after digging yams, tubers or tree roots from the ground, you must cover up the hole you've dug. This assists the plant to regrow; the roots or stems are left underground to help with reshooting, and they can be harvested again. Filling back the soil also ensures that it does not dry out and make it harder for vegetation to grow. Having good native vegetation cover holds the ground surface in place and promotes better soil health. This cover also means there is plenty of food for people and animals.

The skin is the most important organ of the human body and that is also the case when it comes to Mother Earth, but since colonisation, mismanagement of Country has led to bad soil health. When a bulldozer pushes down trees and scrapes the ground surface to bare dirt, it leaves a scar that's like gravel rash on our skin. Eventually the wound can heal and bushland will be healthy again. If the ground is scraped around 30 centimetres deeper, the scar might not heal for a very long time. When massive holes are excavated into the flesh of Mother Earth, it causes deep wounds that will never heal completely. They will be scars on the land forever, just as bad scars remain on our skin for the rest of our lives.

Once the landscape's surface is dramatically changed, it will be difficult to restore what evolution took thousands of years to create. In order to heal Country, tree planting is the first thing that comes to people's minds, and there are carbon programs that aim to plant millions of trees to save the planet. Sometimes planting trees works well, while in other situations it can create a catastrophe.

One time I was doing a cultural burn with an Indigenous community in Australia to help restore a patch of their traditional lands. It was a beautiful place, with gum trees and lots of grassy understorey. It wasn't long before I noticed that a tree-planting group was working on the same block of land. The two groups were applying different solutions in the same place at the same time, and the programs were not complementing each other very well. All I could see were hundreds of plastic tree guards throughout the bush, protecting the young she-oaks that the group had planted. The fact was that there were enough trees on the block already and they were all species indigenous to that place.

We were not allowed to burn in the area where the she-oaks were planted because the fire would burn the plastic guards. Also, it would kill most of the she-oak saplings because they don't like fire at all. A fire-sensitive species had been planted in the wrong fire-dependent system, not where it belonged. It grows naturally in sandier ecosystems, in harmony with fire. I respectfully explained to the group planting the trees that she-oak trees did not come from that area and that it was a eucalypt ecosystem. If the she-oaks flourished, they could take over and destroy the biodiversity of that Country. They could crowd out the gum trees and create a thick understorey, eventually covering the ground with their needle leaves, which would suppress the native vegetation and ultimately affect the soil identity. Planting the she-oaks didn't make sense in this area. I tried to tell them, but the group didn't seem ready to listen. So, it was best to leave them be and walk away.

On another occasion I came across a similar situation when we were burning in the same place as tree planters. This time they were planting a variety of species and once again plastic tree guards were littered throughout the landscape. I know tree guards do serve a purpose, but to me they were an eyesore in the natural bushland.

I met the people doing the work and walked with them while burning patches of land. They were a good crew and one man showed me the trees they were planting. He started to complain about the kangaroos in the area that had completely eaten some of the young trees. 'We need to cull the kangaroos,' he said, as we walked over to an empty plant guard that had been raided.

'Why do you want to kill them when they are just living on their own Country?' I asked.

Not far from where we were standing, I saw three young eucalypts that were originally from that ecosystem. They had grown on their own naturally, and they looked vibrant and healthy. I pointed them out to the man and said, 'Notice how the kangaroos didn't eat those trees. Why do they eat your trees but they don't eat the trees that belong here?'

The man couldn't give me an answer as he stared at the native saplings. I went on to say that the kangaroos know that the planted trees are not from the area and that is why they eat them. The knowledge of Country has been with the animals for thousands of years. 'It is a foreign species to this place, so maybe they see it as a threat,' I explained.

The parent trees in the area were perfectly healthy and grown by nature completely free of charge. No one had to buy the plants, dig the holes or water the saplings, and the trees didn't need plastic plant guards. In many cases all that's needed to repair much of the devastated landscape is effective stewardship to assist nature's own healing abilities.

Cool burning activates the soil so the native vegetation can flourish, but when working with sick Country it is helpful to apply the good fire for a few seasons before diving into major tree-planting operations. Too often, modern humans alter the land and its habitat to what they think is good for it, rather than what the land, the animals and even Indigenous people need for their restoration. In this case, we have to give the land time to respond to the burns and find its own way to recover naturally. As the soil's health improves, trees from the area are likely to reshoot. Knowing the right temperatures to apply to the ground and which will produce the right types of ash comes from precision fire management. Burning the native grasses helps to create an even blanket of black ash that helps fertilise and cleanse the soil. It is natural biochar for the ground.

In Canada, I have seen a method of major tree-planting operations in wildfire-ravaged areas that I have witnessed in Australia too, in forestry plantations across much of our landscape. These operations are based on mass planting and other methods that the major forestry companies use. They run a bulldozer with a ripper on the back across thousands of hectares of land. The result is thousands of trenches scarred across the natural landscape, in rows around 60 centimetres apart and about 50 centimetres deep. Those trenches take a long time to fill up again, particularly in the harder, rocky ground. The soils are overturned, creating dry mounds on either side of the trenches that are almost impossible for the native grasses to grow in. Huge rocks are dislodged and tree roots are left sticking up from the ground. The rocky dirt that had been under the topsoil for so long now sits exposed on the surface. Tree species that can be used for industry are mainly chosen, and rarely are trees planted that belong in the soils in that area.

At the place I visited, the rate of trees surviving was low and the ones that did were yellow in colour and didn't look healthy. Trees were growing quite well in some areas, but they were not worth the destruction of the soils that came with planting them. Bulldozer tracks were still visible and with so much disturbance, the ground's surface was bare. We fire-managed some Country next to these scarred landscapes every season for four years and the results spoke for themselves. We tried to burn in the ripped areas but didn't have much success. The trenches stopped the good fire from restoring the health of the soils for years to come.

The planted area where we were applying fire had been sitting there for eight years with no improvement to the biodiversity. We tried walking along to burn in between the rows but the damage to the land made it unsuccessful. Piles of timber pushed up by the bulldozers to clear the land caught fire, making hot spots that over-cooked the soils. This left white ash that puts the wrong type of biochar into the soil for the native plants, slowing their regrowth.

In the adjoining land that hadn't been planted with foreign trees, the outcome was completely different. At first there were no saplings in the area, but many fir trees and aspens started to shoot up in the right soil types, and berries and other medicinal plants began to spread throughout the landscape. In some places the intense heat from the wildfires had left only sparse patches of grass. Nevertheless, with the yearly burns the grasses started to thicken and their healthy roots could bring nutrients to the soil. Burning annually also protected the young fir trees from wildfire.

As the land's health was restored, each year the fire became more manageable, and the burns helped to activate different species of plants. The fires slowly burned away the dead sticks and logs that covered the ground, removing any litter that might have stopped the native plants from growing. The cool fires also ensured that some trees did die through a process of natural selection. The many fir trees that survived continued to grow with more space between them. That is nature's design, instead of planting trees in rows, like a crop. The young trees that survived the cool burns were a beautiful dark green and always looked healthy.

Some Western scientists say that native grasses must be removed when planting trees, so they do not compete with the trees for water. However, this is not the case. We have seen saplings come up everywhere among the grasses in the burn sites we have managed. Trees and grasses have naturally grown together in their own environment for thousands of years – without the grass we cannot restore the health of fire-dependant ecosystems with fire.

Eventually, we could see the different ecosystems start to stand out within this Canadian landscape. We could see the various species of grasses that grew in different soil types, and under those thick grasses, there was a beautiful, rich soil, moist like a chocolate cake. The difference between the two sites was huge and it clearly showed the effects of working with nature rather than against her.

As I said before, in some cases tree planting is beneficial, but the land suffers if the process does not consider the native life that comes from that area. I have a good Aboriginal friend in Western Australia who purchased a sheep farm on his traditional lands. Sheep had over-run that Country for 150 years, making the soils bare and lifeless. The seed bank was gone, so he had to plant trees that came from that area. Years later, he now has a forest and has even done a burn or two to help recover the soils. My friend's experience shows that tree planting is necessary if trying to activate the land naturally.

The biggest challenge of all is dealing with soils that have been flogged by modern humanity time and time again. In some places, nothing will ever grow in those soils again. There are many Indigenous communities surrounded by lands that have been damaged by agricultural practices. Many of these communities strive to heal their Country, regardless of how lifeless the soils are. My dream is that we have the opportunity to support such groups to restore these sick ecosystems.

There is one thing that humankind must never do again and that is to turn beautiful forest landscapes into barren deserts. Until we start the process of healing our damaged soils, we run the risk of major biodiversity decline and agricultural hardship. There is so much to learn from putting our hands into the dirt, and the more we can apply cultural, nature-based solutions, the more we will prosper. The skin of the Earth is the most important part of Mother Nature's body, and we need to start treating her skin just as we would look after our own.

CHAPTER 8

The healthy Country economy

Many of the issues we face as a society today are due to unbalanced economic structures, dominated by corporations and governments seeking to increase wealth. The extraction economy, for example, leads to fragmented landscapes and communities, which I believe amounts to the demise of the natural order. The extraction economy takes from the earth in ways that do not care for the environment; it harms people and the planet, and that damage will worsen if we do not acknowledge and act on it. In cases when people do become concerned about our economic footprint, action is usually taken at the last minute. Mother Nature falls victim to this social structure, and the land and seas become commodities within a system that takes but gives little back.

From traditional knowledge we can learn how to improve our economic structures. No Indigenous society was ever perfect, but many did coexist with nature for tens of thousands of years.

This human achievement has so much to offer if we look at it with an open mind. It may not solve all our problems but finding a nature-based foundation to work from seems like a good idea. The only way to explore this topic is to venture back in time, long before the extraction economy was formed.

Before colonisation, many Indigenous peoples lived across continents for generations. In Australia, there were over 500 nations that spoke their own languages and lived within their own clan estates. They formed their own governance, kinship and trade systems based on natural lore. The economy for Aboriginal people in Australia was based on having a well-balanced Country. The people cared for the environment and, in turn, received the resources to survive. To have healthy land and waters teeming with the jewels of the Earth gave people a rich culture and plenty to bargain with. That rich, well-managed landscape led to a trade system that was one of the earliest forms of economy, ensuring there were plenty of animals, plants and quarries of stone to contribute to the exchange. This abundance supported a culturally rich, nature-based economic structure.

But a thriving Country did more than just help to provide natural resources to support trade. Having prime land also made it possible to maintain a healthy kinship system. One of the things any Elder will proudly share with you, as well as telling you about their family, is the uniqueness of their traditional homelands. I often reflect on my fond memories of a special Old Man who was my mentor and close friend. He was always proud to take people onto his Country and show them how special his land was. It was like watching a king showing guests around his palace filled with gold and silver. When the Elder took people to the special lagoons on his Country, he would give the biggest smile. Then he would boast about the barramundi fish that populated the waterways and point to the flocks of magpie geese wading by the water's edge. 'I have plenty of tucker on my Country,' he would say, and give his high-pitched laugh in excitement. He would tell stories of how other tribes would come for ceremonies on his lands and feast on the traditional foods they had to offer. It was clear that his homeland and all its natural attributes were his greatest assets.

A healthy environment was crucial for the kinship between clans for many reasons. It would be embarrassing to show others a land that was filled with dead trees, dirty waterways and had no animals living on it. A father would not let his daughter marry into a mob that didn't know how to look after their Country. She would find it hard and might even starve, and the family wouldn't want their kin to live that way. Unhealthy landscapes would not produce enough food to support ceremonies, as some were known to be hosted on tribal estates for weeks.

For thousands of generations, a healthy Country relied not only on land management but also on a social structure that was inclusive of maintaining balanced landscapes. Traditional practices were mostly done in a considerate way of caring and honouring people and place. For example, traditional hunting lores, which meant animals could only be hunted in season and in consideration of the breeding cycles, were strongly enforced and there was so much complex knowledge when it came to harvesting animals. Giving plants and animals a rest from seasonal hunting and gathering each year was an important contributor to maintaining balance. To make it more effective, many clans only took certain genders and age groups from the animal populations.

Over time, modern Western land management practices have enforced green zones and national parks that aim to offer animals and plants a place to revive, but they are usually fixed to one area. This makes it difficult for some animals to move from a protected area to then populate and rejuvenate other areas that sadly have been exhausted by human extraction.

An old traditional saltwater man told me a story of how his Ancestors hunted dugong: they would wait for the herd to swim past and then they would take the last one. That last one was always a male because they would allow the female, very young and old dugongs to swim before them as they fed on sea grass. Other Elders from inland Australia have told me stories of hunting kangaroos: they waited for the last fleeing kangaroo to spear, so that the ones that got away first did not see their kin being killed. This practice reduced stress within the kangaroo population and helped make hunting easier next time. Still today, some clans on the coast that eat saltwater turtles will not gut and clean their catch on the beach in front of the ocean where they caught it. Instead, the turtle is taken to the fresh water and prepared there, so the other turtles do not see the butchering of their kin. This practice has grown in part from the fear that the animals would otherwise move away and make themselves harder to find.

It was also accepted that no part of the animal could be wasted or that you would catch more than you needed. If you had too much, you would share it with the rest of the community. Sharing is one of the most generous attributes that comes from many Indigenous cultures. Being greedy will lead to a competitiveness to acquire more than what is needed, while sharing creates fewer problems culturally and socially and puts less stress on the planet.

Indigenous governance demonstrates the fine balance required to ensure the environment thrives alongside humans. The Old People told me stories of serious punishments that would be dealt if traditional lores were broken. Perpetrators were cast out, speared or beaten, and might even be killed for breaking the lores of Country. Although we do not enforce these harsh punishments today, it does show how seriously people respected the rules of Country. The principles and values of traditional lores may also offer ideas for our modern economy. Anything is better than the situation where greed is combined with a lack of knowledge and understanding.

I attended a forum one time to help find an alternative to the extraction of native old-growth logging. The climate crisis had forced industries that were clear-felling native forests into conversations about change. Attending the forum were community representatives from all corners of the region, environmental activists, and climate scientists with strong evidence to convince industries that they needed to improve their practices. The Traditional Owners were also there, in the hope that their aspirations would be heard, while the forestry workers at the forum were ready to fight for their jobs with a passion. Everyone from all sides of the argument was at the meeting, except for the corporate leaders and local politicians. Apparently, they were asked to come along but they had refused the invitation, which was disappointing. The debate for a sustainable economic alternative to logging the region was left to this segregated community to deal with.

The different groups saw each other as the enemy, but all lived in the same area. Tension filled the air as the forestry workers gave their logging presentations and the environmental activists heckled at every opportunity. When a forestry worker spoke about his love for timber and the dollar value from the wood produced from one tree, an activist sitting in the front row yelled out in a blood-curdling voice, 'Murderer!' The forestry man instantly looked uncomfortable and his colleagues sitting in the audience swooped, shouting back at the woman.

Then a young forestry worker stood nervously on stage and pleaded that cutting down old-growth trees was his life. He gave a speech that stole the hearts of the crowd and humanised the debate. Tears ran from his eyes as he said that he was not the enemy and that logging was all he knew to survive. If the logging industry was to stop in his region, then he and many others would have no job to wake up to each morning. Without work, how could he put food on the table for his family, pay the bills and give his kids a start in life?

He said that in some places where native logging had been stopped, many labourers had lost their jobs. Some were so stressed that they experienced mental illness, family violence and in a few cases, people had taken their own lives. The whole crowd was silent as the young man stood before them. It was at that moment the different sides of the community displayed their compassion for each other. In the end, the only outcome was that people respected and saw each other a little more clearly.

The corporate giants take what they need and then leave a mess behind. There are many cases where big companies come in and set up an extraction enterprise in exchange for short-term jobs. Once these industries have taken their fill, the labourers lose their jobs, the local businesses begin to struggle, and Traditional Owners are left with damaged Country and loss of culture.

For most communities, the way to overcome this situation is to initiate an autonomous future. To create initiatives that everyone can see as beneficial at a local level for the long term. Where opportunities are developed by the people from those regions in ways that bring local autonomy and security for the future. Making this happen while allowing the environment to thrive is the Indigenous blueprint that I am striving to demonstrate, regardless of the challenges. These developments need to start from the ground up, led by people from those regions to restore the land, support livelihoods and encourage innovative solutions.

To revive my mother's Country, efforts started with strengthening the Indigenous rangers' restoration work of the environment. Then we set up projects that involved working with the local landholders and farmers to improve the land that feeds their livelihoods. Next, we looked at possible uses for the invasive plants that are causing problems for the economic and environmental wellbeing of the region. We explored ways to remove those plants to improve the land and to open up more opportunities. Landholders from other regions saw what was happening and asked how they could become involved. One property owner was inspired to create a koala restoration project together with the Indigenous land management practitioners. Major development companies and councils engaged with us to improve the management of their environmental offsets. The local schools also became interested in looking after the land, which sparked local community members to get involved in small projects and business opportunities. There are so many more examples of how this type of community engagement can build into giving the land what it needs to help us thrive. This also leads to a layered economic structure where groups within the community support each other.

The farmers save money by improving the fire management on their property, as they no longer have to buy poisons to kill the weeds. The Indigenous ranger program becomes sustainable because of the increasing contract work they are getting from local industries. The council has a low damage bill after wildfires because the lands were managed effectively to be more resilient. Focusing on ensuring that all economic roads lead to healthy landscapes will help lead to less waste and greater productivity.

Maybe it is possible to apply everything we do to supporting the economic foundation of Mother Nature. If she profits first, then we will all prosper. This is the simple philosophy of Indigenous wisdom developed from an ancient worldview. With more diversity comes greater opportunities, which builds a greater capacity for knowledge. There are opportunities to develop collaborative employment programs based on looking after Country while creating resilience. Opportunities to work with the natural environment to improve livelihoods through innovative community enterprises. Every region is different and can build on its own strength while complementing programs in other regions – just as Indigenous clans are different through their own languages and cultural practices but share the same foundation and responsibilities formed by Country.

The other side to this conversation is the question that is asked so often: Is it possible to do any of this in a world that is so far gone? There are many valid concerns: The world is populated with billions of people; how will they all be sustained? The cost of living is so high that many people have to work for the extraction companies because they have no choice. The threat of economic collapse is real.

I believe that these issues are inspiring people to turn back to nature and restore community-based economies, which bring a broader wealth than just money alone. We cannot heal the planet with the economic systems we have now. Returning to the old ways of strong community values and instigating programs to help regions sustain themselves, instead of relying on governments and businesses. Creating a healthy Country economy that comes from ancient knowledge leads to a healthier broader culture.

The barter-and-trade system needs to be restored in communities, but some Western laws take control and profit from everything we do. Communities should be able to set up food programs so we can share produce with each other. Each community should be able to farm their own food and sell it cheaply to their members without government laws getting in the way. Instead, the Western laws and economic systems make it hard for communities to access healthy foods at affordable prices. Let's try to overcome the negative outcomes of these laws and systems and set up programs based on the local economy, where people can thrive in a functional community.

We can bring about change by restoring our local economies while also assisting the natural world around us to thrive. That is the work we are encouraging communities to do today and the vision I hope will inspire the next generations. With the way the world is going, it is time for communities to come together regionally and look after each other in every way possible – food production, housing, employment and more. We need to create a safety net to catch us when current economic systems let us down.

CHAPTER 9

Sharing knowledge globally

Going back to when I first started sharing knowledge with communities from the far north of Australia to the far south, many people thought it wasn't possible to take concepts of fire knowledge from one end of the continent to the other. The continent is huge and has a complexity of diverse climates and landscapes, such as mountain ranges, tropical rainforests, desert plains, saltwater Country, the many woodlands and wetlands, to name a few. This diversity seemed to convince people that sharing knowledge was not possible.

But as my greatest mentor told me, sharing and applying this knowledge across this amazing spectrum of natural wonders is possible through understanding the principles and indicators of reading Country through the Aboriginal fire lens. Although each region is unique, there is still the underlying foundation of being the same but different, which reveals relationships between landscapes and cultural understandings. This process has helped to rebuild traditional fire regimes that are the right fit for each individual place and the distinct seasons of that area. I've found that cool burns have produced similar results in many different ecosystems across Australia.

Sharing knowledge around Australia to revive traditional land management practices has been an amazing experience. I also know that we can learn from cultures and landscapes far away from our own. That process can help rebuild connections and refine cultural solutions to the challenges we face in our own backyards. With this in mind, I have always had a deep desire to explore traditional practices on a global scale. That opportunity came along in 2018, when I was invited to work with the Indigenous people of the Yunesit'in and Xeni tribes from the Tsilhqot'in Nation in British Columbia, Canada. The project was supported by the Gathering Voices Society, which is an Indigenous unit of the University of British Columbia.

It was the beginning of April when I landed in Vancouver and then caught a domestic flight north to a place called Williams Lake. I tuned into the local news and weather to find that the Western fire authorities had just put a fire ban across the state. I was a little concerned about this and wondered how it would affect the work we had planned to do. When I studied the landscape, I saw snow on the mountains and patches melting on the lowlands, and I wasn't sure why there was a fire ban with so much snow still around. I jumped into a massive pick-up truck from a hire place and set off.

I finally arrived at the Xeni Indigenous reserve, which was the first community I had been asked to work with. It felt like driving into our own Aboriginal settlements back home in Australia.

There were houses with old broken-down cars out the front and horses running around the place, dirt roads everywhere, and no reception at all on my mobile phone. Nothing different here, I thought with a smile, as I parked at the community band office. Not knowing anyone was a bit of a challenge, but I headed in to find someone who could help me out.

When the opportunity came to meet the Chief of the community, it was an honour to talk with him about the fire work ahead. It wasn't long before I mentioned to the Chief that there was a fire ban set across the state. I asked him, 'How is this going to affect the work we are going to do?' He replied with words that I am not used to hearing back home.

'This is our native land,' he said. 'The white man's law does not apply here; it is our lore. You go ahead and do what you need to do.'

I was a little surprised because at home the government interferes with how we want to manage our Indigenous homelands. Not all native communities in Canada have that autonomy, but I was fortunate to be working with the ones that had governance over their homelands. The work that needed to be done would never be completely fulfilled otherwise.

I walked out of the office onto the street and saw the local people checking me out, some with nice smiles and others who seemed curious about who this stranger was. Perhaps they were wondering how this Australian fella could tell them anything when he doesn't even have snow in his country? I understand that curiosity and hesitancy are natural parts of human nature no matter where you go, but I was also aware that I was in a very different landscape. My insecurities eased a little when I met the small crew of three men who would work with me to start the traditional fire program. They stood in front of me, looking a little nervous, as we made our introductions.

'Can you tell me what you know about fire?' I asked, to try to ease the tension.

'Yeah, we know about fire,' one man said. 'Come and we will show you.'

We walked across a cold, muddy dirt road and through a gate, only to stop in front of a shipping container sitting in a yard. They fiddled around with a bunch of keys and the padlock until finally the door creaked open. I peered inside to discover a couple of rakes, shovels, axes and three piss tanks, which are water backpacks for putting small fires out.

'This is our fire equipment,' a man said, as he waved his hand around proudly. 'We thin the trees by cutting their lower branches off and we also fight the fires.'

I immediately realised that they were talking about fire from a Western perspective, so I politely reframed my question.

'I don't mean that kind of fire management. Do you know about the traditional ways of managing the land with fire?'

It turned out that the men knew little about the old fire traditions, as that type of fire management was rarely used anymore. But I was sure that some traditional knowledge would be alive and well somewhere in the community. They mentioned that a few of the Elders in the village would remember things and that gave me a little more hope. Turning away from the container, I looked around at the land that was so unfamiliar to me and wondered how I could move things forward. I didn't know any of the trees or much about the snow seasons, which meant I had to learn a whole new environment. I asked if they could take me out on their land to teach me the names of trees and their cultural relationships.

The men suggested we pick up an Elder who was well known for having cultural knowledge of the land. The Old Man was happy to help and jumped in the truck with us to drive along muddy roads to meet the trees. The first ones they took me to were the poplars. They were thin, medium-height trees, and I noticed that the place where they were growing had well-drained, sandy soils.

I knelt down to pick up a handful of sand to find out how easy it would be to dig into. Nice and clean, I thought, as I let the sand run loosely through my fingers onto the ground. Scattered around were a few different types of berry plants and herbs, similar to the food and medicine plants in our sandy Country back home.

The Elder showed me the Kinnikinnick berry bush that grew low along the ground and pointed out the juniper bush and other traditional plants that were growing in the system. It reminded me of our bloodwood Country, which has similar sandy soils and a diversity of medicinal food plants. In Australia we refer to sandy systems as medicine Country, but on that land in Canada I saw trees and forest-floor plants that were completely different from what grows in Australia. Finally, I inspected the grasses that grew there and saw that they were similar in size and body to our bloodwood grasses. The grass revealing itself through the melted snow was dry and brown, and judging by the slight warmth it seemed that it was ready to burn. I inspected where the poplar trees met the common pine and noticed that the grass there was sparse due to damage by livestock. The rest of the poplar system was boarded by gullies covered with moist leaf litter that looked like a good natural firebreak.

I wanted to find out if the native grass around the poplar trees would burn and go out at these natural firebreaks. I explained this plan to the team and how it related to the way we burned different Country types back home using natural firebreaks. Then I asked if they wanted to light the grass to see if the theory would play out as expected. They seemed a little nervous but then the Elder gave his approval.

'Go ahead, you give it a try,' he said. 'See if it takes off and burns everything down,' he added with a chuckle.

As the laughs settled, I bent down and lit grass for the first time on Canadian soil. It burned beautifully – nice and low – and the fire trickled its way around the poplar ground until it went out at the natural firebreaks.

'I thought it might have been too cold to light,' the Elder said in a shy low tone.

I gave a hopeful smile. It felt as if we were on our way to learning and sharing knowledge from worlds apart. Dry grass can burn in very low temperatures, unlike other types of dead vegetation. We were burning between minus-5 and 5 degrees Celsius that day, but the grass was dry and it burned as expected. After that first demonstration we started burning similar areas that had roads and natural firebreaks around them.

The Elder was walking along lighting the grass here and there with a cigarette lighter. There was one moment when he stopped to watch the fire and looked through the smoke at his homeland. I could see that he was in deep thought. His energy drew me to walk over and ask if he was okay. His watery eyes reflected a mix of pain and joy, and he told me a story that was tragic but beautiful.

'The last time I saw our Elders light fire on the land like this was when I was a little boy. That day I watched the police come and arrest them for burning our land. They took them to jail. Now I am here, 50 years later, lighting these fires today. It's good to be free to burn the land again.' After that, he walked on, continuing to light the grass and watching the fire travel across his Country.

The more the Old Man and I walked around sharing knowledge and stories of the same old problems, the more similarities and connections were revealed between our two distant worlds. It was nourishing for my mind, heart and spirit, and it was like the times I'd spent learning with my Kuku-Thaypan mentors in the earlier days, Poppy and Old Man TG. I thought about the struggles we went through in the 1990s, trying to get fire back on Country. Implementing cultural fire with the Canadian communities was like starting this challenging process all over again.

From what I have heard and learned from other countries, Indigenous communities are all following identical storylines of hardship starting from colonisation. Some communities still face physical violence over the dominance of the resources on their lands. Some may be ahead of others in progressing where we all need to be in harmony, and in some areas that work has not even started. Maybe that is because colonisation disrupted Indigenous cultures at different stages of our histories.

Nevertheless, I was able to share good advice about how we got through such dilemmas back in Australia. The challenge of trying to convince mainstream society and government to listen to Indigenous ways of thinking in Australia has been like trying to break through a brick wall. I've achieved some successful outcomes, but I have certainly encountered a few hurdles along the way, and I would not wish the same experience on the Indigenous people of any other nation. So, it is a blessing to be able to help other communities overseas to avoid the pain of going down the same road.

It would be ideal to find a way globally to help each other catch up, so we are all moving ahead together. The problems of destructive wildfires, floods and every other disaster that affects us socially and environmentally are on all our doorsteps. Not only do we need to deal with them locally, but we should endeavour to understand solutions on a collective level. We can learn so much and generate a greater hope for our futures if we know how to relate to each other and our planet. There is no better way to do this than to go back to our collective roots, when our cultures were connected to Country. For many Indigenous peoples around the world, their cultural knowledge has almost been lost. When I am working with Indigenous communities in any part of the world, the work is not just about fire or any single outcome – it is really about the process of reviving knowledge from landscapes. Cultural knowledge combined with the language of the land can help restore this connection.

As a cultural practitioner I always refer to my Knowledge Triangle to follow the living process of knowledge. There are three points to reviving knowledge that align with the natural world that we are a part of: language, practice and Country.

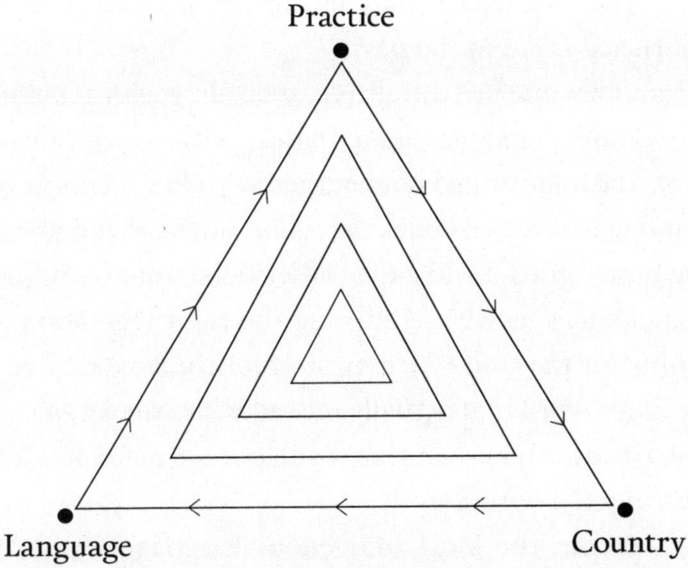

The Knowledge Triangle

When we apply fire for the first time in a place and it goes out where we expect it to, that is the Country telling us it is true. The traditional foods shoot back, the animals return and other cultural indicators occur to confirm that it lines up as the right practice. The land needs the practice of cultural fire so that it can respond and contribute to reviving the knowledge.

Using language brings in the words from the Ancestors who lived with their landscapes for thousands of years. In some cases, language can indicate a place's original identity. A Traditional Owner once told me the language name of a place that meant 'big forest'. When I looked at that landscape recently, there was barely a tree growing there and it was so sad to see. A few old, crooked trees were still standing and that was only because the loggers didn't want the trees that weren't straight. The soil was the right type for the local parent trees, so no doubt a big forest had flourished there in the past.

With another case in Australia, I was burning with a community on their Country and we had a linguist with us who knew the language. The linguist had not engaged with fire practices before and that day he learned about the white smoke that comes from burning native grass. Unlike the black smoke from a wildfire, the white smoke tells us we are burning the right vegetation and it is cleansing for the land. The man suddenly became excited as he knew a single word that actually meant 'white smoke'.

'We have always known this word, but we never knew what it meant,' he said with a smile.

That word in the local Indigenous language was brought back to life with the help of Country and practice, as the three together – language, Country, practice – revived knowledge. Working with the land and joining the dots with the original knowledge is a magical way to get to the big picture. The same thing happened with the Elder in Xeni, Canada, after we had that first burn on his Country that day. The practice sent him home that night with his mind ticking from the experience that had sparked memory.

It helped him to remember a single word in his ancient tongue that meant 'to burn the land'. That word was validation that his people did burn the land to manage it with fire for generations. When he shared the word with the crew and me his eyes lit up with happiness, and I could see that he was keen to get back on the land to light up the grass.

I now truly believe that sharing knowledge from one side of the world to the other is possible. It can reveal so much more of the connectedness that we have with nature and each other. It also further validates that people are a part of nature and not separate from it, as many believe today. We can increase our efforts to save our planet by finding our commonalities within our natural world. In the end there is nothing more satisfying than seeing the wellbeing of the people improve through the process of reviving knowledge from landscapes. The dream is to share this process with more cultures, communities and countries, to gather further insights into who we really are. That is the gift we all need of connecting back to Country, to uncover the blueprints of humanity's connection with creation.

CHAPTER 10

The spark in the duff

I was staying at a guesthouse on an old farm and woke to a cold but beautiful Canadian morning. After breakfast, I jumped into the pick-up truck and headed to the reserve to spend another day with the Xeni crew. During the short drive, it started to snow very lightly, which reminded me how far away I was from the sunburnt country, Australia. When I reached the community band office, the members of the small fire crew were standing there waiting patiently. After our greetings we set off once again to learn more about the different types of Country.

'We are going to take you to the spruce forest,' the Elder said, as we drove down a muddy road.

They led me into the forest where the spruce lived; it was cold, wet and quite dark in among the trees. There was still snow on the ground and the trees stood tall and mystical. The Elder explained that they didn't light fires here because it burns underground if it gets dry enough and the fire can be hard to put out.

On the forest floor there were lots of dead pine leaves and sticks that naturally covered the ground. Under the top layer of fine pine needles was a thick deposit of duff, almost a metre deep. Duff is broken-down bits of leaves and bark that have turned into fine particles over many years. Unlike soil, duff will slowly smoulder if it comes in contact with fire when dry.

The Elder went on to say that his Ancestors burned off the dead wood in the spruce forest in winter, when the ground was frozen and the forest was covered in snow. During that season they could burn the dead wood and branches in the lower sections of the forest without igniting the hazardous duff below. This burn helped to clean up the forest and the fire was also used for cultural practices of encouraging certain food and medicinal plants to grow. Learning that traditional knowledge helped me to understand the spruce and fire relationship a little better.

I noticed that native grasses didn't grow in the forest because of the heavy pine needle cover on the ground. The spruce was proving to be the same as our no-fire Country back home. Usually, trees growing in ecosystems where leaf litter is naturally found on the forest floor do not like fire. They are sensitive to any level of heat and will become sick or die if fire enters the area. In the spruce forest, the duff meant double trouble if fire was to enter the ecosystem. Not only is the fire bad for the wellbeing of the trees, but the duff allows the fire to travel underground to cause bigger problems down the track. This can certainly happen if fire comes at the wrong time – that is, in the dry, warmer months, after the snow and ice have melted.

This made me think about how we burn certain landscapes in Australia to protect fire-sensitive ecosystems within the traditional fire window. We have to consider all the land types and their relationships with fire, to ensure we put the fire in the right place at the right time to care for all adjoining ecosystems. In Australia, we burn the landscapes around the no-fire Country in the season when the land is not flammable. So we decided to try burning the fire-dependent ecosystems next to the spruce forest in the hope of achieving similar results in Canada.

We drove off to find more grassy areas and walked the land, burning some good-sized grassy patches within stands of common pine. Right next to us was a large lake that still had solid ice at the shoreline. In the burn area was a small patch of spruce and I noticed that the fire was going out at the edge. The ground was soggy and I could see that the fire had no way to get in. This indicated that it was possibly the right time to burn the surrounding landscape to protect the spruce. So far, so good, I thought, as we went along our way, burning the grass.

On another day we came to a spruce forest that was a little higher in elevation than the others we'd visited, and it was also drier. I could tell that the area had not had a good winter season, as there was little snow showing in this spruce patch.

'Be careful not to let the fire in this bit of spruce,' I called out to a couple of the young men in our team. Seeing that all was well, we continued to burn the grass and enjoy the day. We were able to burn effectively, carefully keeping the fire out of the sensitive landscape.

Not long after that, the youngsters mischievously lit up a huge pile of logs that sat on the edge of the spruce. I turned around and saw what looked like a bonfire, but I was not too concerned – that was until the fire grew hot enough to spread into the spruce forest and a tree went up in flames. There was a massive roar, like jet engines starting up, as the whole tree burned savagely right to the top. The inferno flared, pushing the flames above the canopy, over 6 metres into the air. It looked terrifying as the fire caught onto another tree that went up the same way.

I was surprised by the flammability of this tree. By now, the young men were freaking out and didn't know what to do when the massive flames roared again and the fire engulfed another tree. I stood and watched the flames dancing high in the air and started to talk to the fire quietly in my mind, 'Settle down now. What are you teaching me?'

The flaming trees eventually calmed down until there was just a small fire on the forest floor. But it trickled slowly along the ground to the next tree, and the massive flare-up started all over again. By now this was really scaring the young fellows and they went into full panic mode.

'Let's call the wildfire service,' one of them yelled out.

'No, don't even think about it,' I yelled back. 'We stick together as a team.'

We grabbed the piss tanks from the truck and got them ready to go. With water packs on our backs, we stood there watching a fourth tree flare up, pushing the flames high into the sky.

'It's okay,' I said. 'Wait for the flames to go down again. When they do let's move in and put them out.'

The Elder was calm, which was helpful for me because the young men were trembling in their shoes.

'This is what happens when the spruce catches on fire,' he said softly, while watching the flames dancing high above the trees.

When the flare settled down once more, we scurried into the forest to aim water at any fire travelling on the ground. We managed to put out the fire and stop the flames from reaching another tree. It was a relief for all of us, as the drama had certainly shaken the crew up a little.

'Well, there is another lesson about the spruce,' I said. 'Never pile logs and old fuel next to this type of forest. That fire would not have gone in there if it wasn't for that pile of logs at its doorstep.'

The Elder nodded in agreement, and we continued burning for the short time we had left that afternoon. The spruce trees were incredibly flammable in the cold temperatures. It certainly confirmed for me that it was no-fire Country. The colder the land, the more flammable it is, because of the high content of oils in the vegetation. We have trees in Australia that go up in flames too, but not like the spruce tree.

The following day was my last with the community; the next leg of the trip was to travel to meet the Yunesit'in community, an hour's drive away. The last day was a little more relaxed because I didn't like to burn Country and then leave on the same day. We hung around the band office for a while until I decided to drive out to our burn areas from the previous day for one last inspection. I was on my own this time, as it was just going to be a quick check-up to fill in some time. As I drove along the dirt road, admiring the burned patches we'd achieved, I came to the spruce forest where the drama had occurred. A couple of trees were scorched to death from the fire and seeing them like that was disappointing.

Looking closer, I noticed streams of smoke oozing out through the canopies. It seemed a bit eerie, so I pulled the truck over and walked in to have a closer look. When I got inside the forest, I couldn't believe my eyes – it was like a scene from *The Lord of the Rings*. The smoky forest floor looked almost like bubbling lava as steam shot up everywhere. The duff had caught alight and there was a fire quietly smouldering underground. Two more trees had fallen down because their root systems had burned out completely. There were no flames anymore, but the boiling duff was extremely hot and alive. I stepped back and landed right on a patch of burning duff, which made the soles of my new boots instantly melt away. This was the only time I wore steelcap boots; it was my first visit to Canada, and I wanted to protect myself from the cold. I think the spirits made me wear the boots on this rare occasion, so I didn't burn my feet.

It was clear that the fire would burn underground for weeks and the summer months were not far away. I drove back to find the team and we returned with piss tanks to put out the hot spots in the duff. We quickly discovered that spraying water on them was useless; we needed proper water tanks and hoses. The community had no firefighting unit, and it seemed the only option was to call one in.

'We have an old water pump back at the community. We could pump water from the lake to put it out,' the Elder suggested.

This sounded like the best option at that moment, so a couple of the crew went back to fetch the water pump.

When it arrived, the pump looked so old it was almost an antique, with the paint nearly all stripped off. But as long as it worked, that was all that mattered. The Elder walked out onto the icy edge of the lake and put the hose into the freezing water. The pump sputtered and sparked until the motor finally began chugging along. We had two hoses running off the little old engine and the water came gushing out at full flow. As it hit the duff, explosions of ash spewed out of the ground from the impact of the cold water hitting the extreme heat. Dirt and mud spat into the air and would have hit us in the face if we were not careful.

Even pumping from a massive lake into this sizzling pot was not enough to put out the fire underground. We had to dig into the duff with shovels to get the water into the right place, otherwise it was a useless exercise. Once we thought the fire was out in one place, wisps of menacing smoke came up from other areas of the forest floor. Digging into the leaking signs of smoke revealed another large glowing hotspot burning underground that was fascinating and annoying at the same time. We pumped the water continuously until the late afternoon, finally putting out the smouldering duff.

'I will never let fire get into that spruce Country or any duff situation again, that is for sure,' I said to myself.

The Elder told us that these hotspots can burn in the ground under the snow all the way through winter. The fire can pop up again in the drier seasons to create a wildfire later in the summer. A spark in the duff can be devastating for the spruce trees and can bring destruction to the forest. The team took me to visit another spruce forest that had suffered from a fire a couple of years earlier. The story was that it had started from a campfire in the warmer months and had destroyed a large area of spruce.

We stood on a hill overlooking the dead forest and it made me sad to see the layers of fallen trees. There was not one living tree left standing and there would not be for a long time. The place was a mess of tangled logs suppressing any new growth from coming up from the ground. The dead timber would take many years to break down before a new forest could grow again. The vegetation from this fire-sensitive area may or may not recover eventually. Either way, it will struggle if it does not receive the stewardship it needs.

It is the same for our no-fire Country in Australia. Once you burn trees in these systems, it takes a long time to bring those types of forest back again, and in colder countries the regrowth is even slower. Some ecosystems that are sensitive to fire might never come back at all and that would be a great loss to the planet. With wildfires becoming more frequent in these places, the chance for forests to regrow faster than the rate of decline dwindles even more.

The spruce trees reminded me of our big river red gum forests back home in the lagoon and water Country. Many of our river red gum forests in Australia used to sit in water most of the time and held water around their feet permanently. Companies and individuals pumped the water out for agriculture and mining, leaving the river red gums high and dry, surrounded by duff. You cannot put fire into river red gum systems that are choked up with duff. I saw that the same thing happens in Canada; the fire goes into the ground and burns out the roots, causing 500-year-old trees to fall over from what started as a single spark.

It makes me want to cry when this happens to old trees. They are vulnerable, with no water left to protect them and no management of the fire-prone systems around them. In these cases, it is not about putting the fire back on the Country; the proper answer is to bring the water back. Convincing mining companies and farmers to put the water back in these places will be harder than getting cultural fire on the land. Nevertheless, the water is something we need to fight for to support many of our natural wonders.

In northern Australia, we have lost ancient fire-sensitive forests that will never return to their original state. I am thinking about the places where the boab tree grew in dry rainforests among unique animal and plant species. Now those trees and animals are all wiped out due to bad land management. A beautiful forest formed over millennia has become a massive infestation of lantana and other weeds. I call it upside-down Country because the trees look like they are upside-down – and this can happen to any ecosystem. Their dead branches look like their roots rising into the air, while the thick growth of invasive plants and the dead vegetation on the forest floor is like the canopy.

These forests existed alongside Aboriginal occupation for tens of thousands of years and now they have gone. There is a place called Forty Mile Scrub on Ewamian Country in North Queensland, and it saddens me every time I pass it while driving out to our neighbouring Tagalaka homelands. My youngest son, who hadn't seen the forest before it was destroyed, was in the car with me one day. I tried to explain to him what the forest used to look like and I found it disturbing. I wanted to create a picture for him of a beautiful place, and I could see him trying to imagine big healthy fig trees and a lush jungle while we were looking at a dead and degraded landscape. It made me wonder how many more parents will have to describe to their children what nature looked like before it was destroyed by modern society.

In southern Western Australia, I have worked in forests of white gum trees that are a fire-dependent landscape. Some parts of that land had not been burned for decades, as the natural bushlands are surrounded by farming crop lands. As a result, thick layers of duff had formed around the bases of the tree trunks in many parts of that Country. There should never be any duff in these fire-prone ecosystems. When I saw it, I told the fire crew to rake it away from the trees before we burned. I explained that we needed to burn the duff to expose the soil so the native vegetation could grow again. The duff was only about 5 centimetres deep, but it was enough to cause damage and set fire to the old parent trees.

After we burned away the layers of dead leaf litter and duff that day, we put out any smoking logs and went home for the night. The next day we came back to find a perfectly healthy tree had fallen to the ground and was on fire. The crew was devastated as they had missed the layers of duff around this tree. I walked around and showed them a few other trees that still had duff smouldering on the ground near their trunks. The crew raked around them, but the duff was deeper than they had thought.

'All these trees with the duff still around them will die unless we rake it away now,' I explained.

Smoke was rising from the ground everywhere and just as in the spruce forest in Canada, we had to spend all day putting the fire out. The crew worked hard in the hotspot areas, raking and dousing water from their firefighting unit. It was a valuable lesson that made them realise how much work needs to be done to restore and protect the forests on their homelands. Having duff form in fire-dependent ecosystems is a sure sign of over

100 years of neglect and mismanagement. The forests in these areas need to be carefully restored so the right fires can be reintroduced and biodiversity can thrive.

As for no-fire Country like the river red gums in Australia and the spruce in Canada, we need to protect them by managing the fire Country landscapes around them. We must burn at the right time when these sensitive landscapes can keep the fire out, and that is all part of mosaic burning, which is central to cultural burning techniques. The only way to look after any forest is to manage all the different ecosystems that surround it, and no doubt it's the same for other fire-sensitive landscapes anywhere in the world. In a time when climates are getting drier, it is crucial to protect these systems before they are lost forever.

CHAPTER 11

The fir and the aspen

After visiting the Xeni homelands in Canada, I set off on the short drive to the Yunesit'in community in the Tsilhqot'in Nation. I was looking forward to seeing different Country and working with another group of people. The mountainous landscape that surrounded this community was destroyed by wildfire in 2017 – a year before my first visit. I'd seen it on the news in Australia and to experience the aftermath firsthand was devastating.

In places where tall pine forests once grew, dead trees resembling burned matchsticks were now littering the land. It was hard to believe that a lush forest had flourished there until quite recently. It was similar to the devastated landscapes back home after such fires, but this was one of the worst cases I had seen. My aim on this visit was to work with the community to build their traditional knowledge and to improve the condition of the land after the wildfires. I wanted to see if the restoration methods we use in Australia to revive bushfire-damaged landscapes could also be used to help the Canadian landscapes.

As I drove on, I came across areas where the local logging companies had completely ripped the dead trees from the land, ravaging the last harvest of timber before it started to rot and spoil. The Country was a huge mess of churned-up soils, left dry and disturbed by the impact of the earth-moving machinery. Dead stumps and tangled logs covered a neglected wasteland. That devastation gave me a sad view of the deterioration we are facing across the globe.

I pulled into the Yunesit'in band office and received a warm welcome from some of the admin staff. Russell Ross, who was the Chief of the reserve at that time, was also there to greet me. Russ is passionate about finding cultural ways to heal his community and Country following the infernos that devastated his homelands. It seemed that everyone was keen to get started.

We only had a small team but there were enough people to do the important work that was needed. The first place we lit up was along the beautiful Chilcotin River, with its fast running glacier waters. This river system had supported the spring salmon season for generations, but now its banks were choked with thick, dry grass that made it hard to access the river. The Yunesit'in crew wanted to clean up the riverbanks with a burn so the community could come down during salmon season to scoop the fish up with dip nets. Clearing along the river would also make it easier to see snakes, which were a concern to some of the people.

After our visit to the river, we went on to burn the grassy hillsides that surrounded the community. The main aim was to

A black bear climbing a dead fir tree in Country devastated by the 2017 wildfires in Yunesit'in, British Columbia, Canada. Photo by Hamish Hamilton.

try to restore the native grasses across the land to help repair the damaged soils.

'That is what we want after the burn, to see that the grass stocks are still there, nice and green,' I said, brushing off the black ash on the ground to reveal a carpet of fresh grass underneath. 'This will replace the old dry grass, so that the animals will come and feed on it.'

The team was excited about that. Since the wildfire, it had been hard to find deer close by the community.

We continued burning while one of the men sang traditional songs and did a happy dance to acknowledge the land and the Ancestors. It felt good to burn while listening to him chant away, kicking up the dust with his work boots. His songs echoed

Burning to restore damaged landscapes with Russell Ross on his traditional homelands on Yunesit'in Country, Canada. Photo by Josh Nuefeld.

through the landscape as the low fire crackled at a slow pace beside him. We joked around while we sprinkled fire around the landscape. Sometimes this is how things get done, and it helps to move away from the seriousness that often consumes our lives.

I looked up at the nearby hills that surrounded the community, where the dead trees stood above the torched, brown landscape. It was time to visit those rocky hills, to see how the land there had responded to such intense heat. As I scrambled to the top of a hill, I saw there was no vegetation at all, just hard, bare stoney soil. On this rocky hilltop I met the fir trees that had lived up there and grew down the ridge lines to the lowlands. The area reminded me of our ironbark Country in Australia. Most of our ironbark trees grow in the same sandy soils and populate much of the stoney mountain Country. These hard stoney ecosystems in Australia are referred to as storm-burn Country, because a lot of rain is needed for the vegetation to grow back after the fire. The Old People at home told me that you should never burn these areas when the ground is dry. Otherwise, the vegetation will take a long time – sometimes decades – to grow back again. Burning when the land is dry can cause problems ranging from no longer providing food and habitat for the animals to bad soil erosion. In the hills near the Yunesit'in community, the topsoils had washed into the river systems.

Panning the view, I saw a small group of fir trees on the lower ridges that were still alive and well. I went down and stood close to one big old tree and ran my fingers over the rough bark. The design and feel were almost identical to the bark of our ironbarks back home: same colour, same deep wavy patterns and steel-like hardness that showed its resilience to fire. I looked up to admire the Elder fir standing before me on Tsilhqot'in Country.

'You remind me of our ironbark tree,' I said. 'It is as if you are related in some ways.'

I looked down and noticed red and blue stones surrounding the base of the trunk. I'd seen very similar stones around the ironbarks too. With a hand on the trunk of the fir tree I thought about the similarities between the trees that were growing so far apart. The ironbark and fir are distant relatives when you look at them from the perspective of traditional knowledge and not through Western ecological views.

By this time, the men had wandered over and I showed them the indicators and shared the story. The men studied the coloured stones but didn't seem very interested. They were just stones in the dirt that they see every day across their homelands.

'I have to take you back home to Australia to show you,' I said. 'Then you will understand what I am talking about. Just as you have various species of fir trees, we have different species of ironbark, and some can be found mixing with the softer, sandier and darker soil types.'

The narrow-leaved red ironbark is one species often found in the winter-burn ecosystems. It can live away from storm-burn Country and grow in richer soils than its rocky Country cousins. The versatility of the fir seemed to be very similar. This hinted at the possibility that it may also have different burning patterns for different soil types, just like the ironbarks. I decided we needed to do some burning within these landscapes to test the knowledge indicators. There was so much work to be done first, but the opportunity to burn the stoney Country would come soon enough.

A few years later in Australia, we held the Custodians of Country Gathering hosted by the Djabugay in northern Queensland. The idea for staging this large cultural event had come from holding many National Indigenous Fire Workshops annually. Two members from the Yunesit'in community, a couple named Anthony and Bec, came to the event. They were excited to travel to Australia for the first time, although they were scared of crocs, snakes and spiders. I had been working with Bec and Anthony on their traditional lands for a couple of years by then and it was great to welcome them to our homelands.

We went for a trip on Country to do some burning and as we approached the ironbark tree, it felt like I was introducing them to an old friend of mine, and it gave me a warm, happy feeling. The land was hilly, hard and rocky and we stopped at the foot of the tree to say hello. 'Here is the ironbark tree, your fir relation,' I said to them, in a formal introduction.

They stood close to the tree and looked straight into the bark, running their fingers over the rough patterns.

'Oh, yeah,' said Anthony. 'It looks and feels just like our fir.' He pinched a bit of bark off and smelled it. 'It smells like our fir too.'

Bec agreed with a smile, and in that moment it was like they were meeting new members of the family.

'Now look at the ground,' I said, while reaching down to pick up the red and blue stones around the base of the tree.

I dropped the stones in Anthony's hand and a look of realisation spread across his face.

'Wow, these are the same kinds of stones too,' he said.

It was good to communicate through cultural landscapes from one side of the globe to the other. We looked up to the canopy, seeing ironbark leaves instead of pinecones and needles.

'Same but different,' I said. 'Same but different.'

Two years later, we brought ten Yunesit'in community fire practitioners to Australia to meet the ironbark trees and the tea-trees too. The next year we took a team of Australian practitioners to Yunesit'in to see the trees and they were amazed by the similarities. Without the work we had done over the years, this exchange would not have been possible. Our Living Knowledge Network is working this way with our partners to build a global exchange program – to raise fire practitioners' knowledge to another level and create meaningful work to support our programs. We can learn so much from the similarities and interrelationships with nature and culture. Everything is connected; that is the principle shared among all life forms within our collective existence.

The following year I went back to the Yunesit'in community to continue training the crews and exploring more Country to get the fires happening. Russ took us to the foot of an escarpment that ran along one side of the village. The escarpment was pretty high and still had snow at the top, which made for the perfect firebreak. The crew walked to the lower section of the mountain and started to light the dry grass. I was pleased to see that we were burning larger areas because that was a sign of the team's growing confidence. The flames were only small as the fires wove around the landscape, while each of the crew members set off in their own direction.

We walked higher up the escarpment to light a fire right next to the snowline at the very top. I found it mesmerising watching the fire gently dance around small patches of melting snow. It was a nice place to take in the view, while standing next to the burning grass to keep warm in the cool air. I spent a little time there before wandering further along the ridge, to find the crew. Realising there was no one around, I walked over to the edge of the cliff to look for them. I could see some of the crew way down below, lighting small fires here and there.

There was still plenty of daylight, so I decided to light some fires further along the ridge before heading down to catch up with the others. It was good to make sure the fire was lit from the top of the mountain so it could gently trickle down into the evening. Walking along lighting the grass with a cigarette lighter, taking in the details of the land, I stumbled across a very shallow gully, where a few dead aspen trees were standing from the last wildfire. I walked towards them, noticing that the soil changed from hard and rocky to wet, dark and sandy once inside the aspen's territory.

It appeared the aspen liked to grow in the moist gullies, which made me think of our tea-trees back home. Tea-trees love moist soils and can also live in sandy areas in gullies and low-line landscapes. The aspens and tea-trees have similar white bark, except the bark on our tea-trees – also called paperbarks – is quite fragile. The aspen's bark is harder, perhaps to cope with the freezing winter temperatures in Canada. I stood next to one of the dead aspens and noticed the dry bark was cracking and flaking off the trunk. I broke off a long strip and ran it through my hands to analyse it.

If this aspen tree is like our tea-tree, I thought, then the bark must light up like a torch, just as our paperbark does. In some places we use the bark of the tea-tree as a torch to light Country and to start small campfires in the wet season. I flicked the lighter to one end of the aspen bark and it instantly caught fire and would not go out. I held the burning bark up in front of me with a big smile on my face, as the flame burned like a candle.

'Ahh, you are like our tea-tree. You two must be related,' I said to the dead trees.

The aspen bark burned more slowly than the bark from our tea-tree, which was a great advantage as it would allow us to carry fire further. I decided to put it to the test. The burning aspen made lighting the grass so easy and it felt like another piece of the puzzle had found its place. The long-burning bark allowed me to light multiple places with little effort and without bending down. There was no need for flicking cigarette lighters or matches and certainly no need for lighting fossil fuels in drip torches. The bark was the proper fire lighter for that landscape and it was among the best I had used. I found that the thinner the bark, the better it was to maintain a constant flame.

I continued further along the ridge, lighting the dry grass, and then noticed that I was on my own. I looked down and saw that the cars had gone. That was the moment to go back because I couldn't keep burning without the people from that Country with me. I had a sudden thought that a bear might wander along and find me there all by myself too. One of the crew had told me that bears were starting to wake from their winter sleep at that time of year. Then my thoughts went to mountain lions, even though I'd heard that attacks were rare in the area.

I would not know what to do if a bear came running towards me, regardless of the advice to stay still to avoid provoking it. Of course, many people in Canada and America would say they are frightened of the dangerous animals in Australia. We have saltwater crocodiles back home but, generally speaking, you have to jump into their murky waters to get eaten. Luckily, attacks are not that common, but it is a fun conversation to have with Canadians when comparing dangerous animals.

It was definitely time to head back down the mountain. After taking a few steps, Norma, one of the crew, appeared through the clouds of grass smoke. She looked at me with surprise on her face. 'I thought there was no one else up here,' she said, sounding relieved.

'I did too,' I replied, sounding just as pleased and surprised.

Norma was looking at the burning bark in my hand, so I walked over to present it to her.

'This must be your burning torch for lighting Country,' I said. As she held up the bark, Norma's face lit up with the dancing flame reflecting in her eyes.

I explained about the fire torch and Norma listened with great interest, so I suggested that she give it a try. She walked along and began lighting up the grass. It was magic watching her connecting with the land this way. I could see it was another natural cultural fit that brought a deeper connection to the ancient practices.

As I was no longer alone, it made sense to collect some more bark and walk the fire with her. We continued along the ridge for another couple of hours, keeping each other in sight. Then we noticed a few of the crew way down at the bottom of the mountain looking up at us. The day was almost over so we took that as our cue to meet up with them. We strolled down with the aspen torches burning in our hands, and the flames caught our crew's attention from afar. The aspen bark was used for burning Country for the rest of the time I was there.

Finding the aspen bark torch for burning on Yunesit'in Country.
Photo by Josh Neufeld.

That night we watched the fire trickle down the massive mountainside, and it looked so beautiful. Everyone from around the district saw that fire and some people even called the Yunesit'in community to check if they were alright. They said, 'We are fine, we are doing cultural burning the old way and we have a guy from Australia helping us.'

I had a little laugh when they told me, but it was great for everyone to see the good fire burning in such challenging times. I knew that it might draw a bit of attention, but it was also a sign that the Yunesit'in were well and truly bringing back their traditional fire.

The next morning, we continued the burning; the fire picked up as the wind increased and stayed that way for the rest of the day. The ridge lines that ran down the mountain were populated with fir trees and the fire trickled along them beautifully. The gullies below the ridge lines were full of large dead aspen forests that had perished in the wildfire years before. Just as with our tea-tree, a wildfire going through these dead tree communities would turn into a very hot fire.

As predicted, the fire entered the dead aspen groves, and it created a raging inferno that gave the crew a little scare. The flames roared high into the sky and dark black plumes of smoke rose into the atmosphere. We knew that the wildfire service was watching and wondering what we were up to because they kept contacting Russ and voicing their concerns.

I sat on a small grassy hill overlooking a large dead aspen patch as the fire settled down to do its job of burning away the old logs. Every few minutes there was a loud, eerie creaking sound when another dead parent tree fell to the ground. One by one, the aspen Elders crashed as burning logs, to join the fire that turned them into ashes to return to the soggy soil. It was like a ritual that was renewing life for the next generations to follow. I closed my eyes and listened to the event unfolding, and it gave me a positive feeling deep down inside. It was as if the aspen trees in the dead forest were grateful for the helping hand to return to the earth, after the wildfire had taken their lives.

I walked a little further down the hill, where young aspen trees in a couple of small gullies were alive and healthy. The forest floor had a thin layer of leaf litter instead of dead trees and grass. Further down the hill was another system that had slightly older trees, with a thicker layer of aspen leaf litter covering the ground. Standing there, I watched as the magic unfolded around these living ecosystems – the fire went out at the edges and did not burn the leaves on the ground.

After seeing that fire, it made sense to me that a healthy aspen forest can act as a natural firebreak in the right seasons. It seemed the right time to burn the fir ridge lines down the mountains, as the aspen in the gullies helped to keep the fire contained. I checked a couple of other living aspen patches and found more evidence of the fire going out at the edges. It was the same behaviour as when we burn the ridge lines of mountainsides back home. Many of the gullies that run down our mountains also have leaf litter ecosystems that don't burn and keep the fires out.

There are special plants in those gullies back home, and we must take great care that they don't die from fire. Keeping the aspen systems healthy in these terrains was a little different, but just as important. The aspens create a natural firebreak to allow the fir trees to have their seasonal burn. I was interested in doing more trials over time to confirm the effectiveness of these firebreaks.

The piles of dead wood had suppressed the new growth, which prevented the ecosystem from fully recovering. I realised that the dead aspen had to burn to clear the debris for the next generation of trees to take their place. The timing for our burn was perfect as the soil in the gullies was freezing cold and soaking wet from the melting snow. This meant that the hottest of fires had no impact on the soil and the trees' network underground was protected. After the intense burn, we inspected the site to find that the soil was cool and rich. The fire was so hot and wild that you would think nothing could survive that kind of temperature. Yet soon after the healing fire, young shoots of aspen started to appear. That was incredible because these trees are fire sensitive and will die from hot fires in the drier times.

The aim from there was to burn regularly at the right time to nurture the young aspen groves, so they would grow and become more effective as they aged. It will take frequent burning during their winter sleep in the early years of their lives to help them reach adulthood.

It was an honour to meet the aspens, firs and spruce in Canada in such a way that I could see close similarities to our trees in Australia. It is evident that Indigenous people globally share similar cultural practices and connections that have evolved with Mother Nature. Although we look different, speak different languages and have our own unique customs, we share many values and responsibilities that align with nature.

I have also grown to learn that trees are just like people. They look different from each other, they live in their own Country, they have their own family groups and they have a responsibility to the natural world. But deep inside they are all trees, just like we are all people, and modern humanity can learn valuable lessons from them. Understanding the trees will help to restore and share ancient knowledge, as they possess so many benefits that hold our entire existence together.

CHAPTER 12

Restoring the knowledge

Following my first visit to Canada in 2018, I have continued to work with Russ and others from the Yunesit'in community. I stay from March to April, when the snow begins to melt. Even now, seven years after the program started, much of the landscape that suffered from wildfires is still covered with dry grass and the trees are still struggling to reshoot. In fact, in places where we did not burn, the land has not changed much at all from the state it was in after the wildfires. But these days when I go back to the community, I am greeted with the sight of white smoke rising in the air, coming from small grass fires that some of the residents have set alight.

On a recent visit, Russ was proud to report that since first taking part in the fire program, the people have been burning around their little community more often. That put a smile on my face; it was good to see them gaining confidence in their cultural burning again. He went on to tell me that their crew had done slightly bigger burns in the foothills of the mountains that surrounded their town.

I was happy to be back in Yunesit'in and settled into the guesthouse to prepare for the next few weeks of burning Country. This time a few more community members joined us, which was another sign of progress. Most of the crew involved at the beginning were women, and they worked alongside Russ to give the program the best start possible. A two-person Canadian film crew, supported by the Gathering Voices Society, have fully documented our work. They did interviews with the Elders, as well as talking with the practitioners about what they were learning and feeling.

At the start of this visit, we all went down to the Chilcotin River again, where we always do our first burns to build confidence and warm up for the season. A couple of Elders came down to be a part of the burns, to share stories and see what it was all about. I had the chance to have a long conversation with Maria Myers, a respected Elder from the community. She was a beautiful spirit, and we talked for some time. Her stories and her knowledge of the land were very similar to the cultural knowledge I had learned from Elders back home in Australia. Talking with her was a grounding experience that reassured me we were on the right track towards cultural revival. Just like all wise and knowledgeable Elders, Maria would come to life when talking about the land. I could see her happiness as she watched the young ones walk with the fire across their homelands. After our conversation I joined the rest of the crew, who were lighting the dry brown grass around a hilly landscape.

There were plenty of fir and aspen trees in the area and they were spaced well apart with open grass cover between them. The grass was sparse because the soils were so damaged from cattle and the recent wildfire. However, burning the old grass created fertile black ash that would help improve the soils. The temperate heat of the fire encouraged native plants to grow back and fill in the gaps in the bare ground between the trees. The crew walked through these areas, lighting spot fires to clean up the land and make way for the new plants to shoot.

Back when I first worked with the Yunesit'in community, they didn't have much firefighting equipment – just shovels and rakes, and eventually a few piss tanks turned up. Today they still haven't got enough equipment, but we are determined that more support will come from all the good work we are putting in. As I watched the crew use their boots to stomp out fire that was trickling outside of the burn zone, I thought about how we traditionally controlled small fires with tree branches back home. The Old Man first taught me that practice in northern Australia when he used a branch from an ironwood tree. They are suitable because their leaves tend to stay on the branches when we're hitting them on the ground with great force. I tested the trees in Yunesit'in Country to try to find the right branch that could be used in the same way. The first attempts didn't work very well, but then I went to a fir tree and noticed that its lower branches snapped off easily, which was a good sign. After I gave it a long battering, the branch still held itself together without losing its fine needle leaves. I swung the fir branch at the fire and it put out the flames quickly and effectively. Of course, the branch would not be suitable for putting out massive fires, but it was very effective for our steady burns.

Plus, we got to trim the lower branches of the trees naturally over time and that is good for them. The community also snapped off branches to sit on inside their traditional sweats (like saunas), which shows their cultural memories of the tree.

I called the crew over to explain the use of the fir branch to put out the fire. Within minutes the whole team was using the branches, and from that moment on, fir branches were part of their fire-management toolkit. Years later, it is still the Yunesit'in cultural burning crew's most used fire tool.

As the days went on, we did a few more small burns and that gave me the confidence to push things a little further. I wanted the crew to experience burning larger areas of natural landscapes, as well as just treating small fields. That was necessary if we were serious about healing the massive territory that made up their traditional homelands. Russ agreed and selected an area just outside of the community that he thought suitable. The property extended down into a large valley towards a creek that looked about a kilometre away. Judging by the landscape, it was ready for a burn, and it would be one that we could easily control.

'Let's do it then,' I said.

The team seemed a bit uncomfortable but eventually drew up the courage to give it a go. There was a moderate wind blowing towards a running creek that I'd decided would be our firebreak. We walked down and started to burn from the creek bank against the wind. We practised a technique of walking along roughly 50 metres and then letting the fire burn back onto the burned land. Like all cultural burning techniques, we had to walk the land to place the fire in the right place, so it did what the land needed it to do.

We burned all day, working with the dancing low flames across the sea of dry grass and wild berries. We spread out, each of us cleaning up the land. I was scanning the ground to study the soils and I saw what looked like an arrowhead. It was a perfect sample, professionally crafted with knapped edges. I picked it up and cleaned it with my fingers to find that it was made from obsidian, a hard, dark volcanic rock. I showed it to Russ and then gently placed the beautiful piece into his hand.

He respectfully held up the arrowhead between two fingers and smiled at it. 'Ah you found another one,' he said. 'These arrowheads were used for hunting in the old times. We have found a few around here before.'

Russ explained that we were on a hunting ground that had been used by his Ancestors for generations. That confirmed for me that before colonisation it was an open grassy landscape, home to animals such as deer, elk and bear, to name a few.

A little further away from where the arrowhead was found, we stumbled across the remains of some old pit houses by the creek. Pit houses were traditional winter dwellings that the Tsilhqot'in Nation dug underground, with logs and earth for the roofs. All that was left of them were large holes in the ground, but even without roofs the pit houses still looked incredible. The place had been a seasonal camp where a family group had stayed long ago, living off the land. It must have been during the times of early colonisation, or even earlier, making the houses hundreds of years old. The Country would have been plentiful then and everything these people needed was all around them.

I found that the cultural stories, artefacts and practice, combined with nature's response to the seasons, were helping me understand this land. I could piece together the key elements of living knowledge to find the practice that reconnects people with Country. That is the formula of the Knowledge Triangle that I mentioned earlier. Every day these findings added another piece to the puzzle to help revive the traditional fire practices for the Yunesit'in community.

Russ took the arrowhead for safekeeping, and we left the pit house site to continue walking with the fire across his homelands. We burned Country into the night, until the job was done. Then we went home to rest while the fire was extinguished in the cold evening air.

The next day we set off to walk the beautiful fire-kissed land to inspect what had and hadn't burned. As soon as we began walking, a herd of deer ran across the hills in front of us, which felt like a great reward for our efforts.

Another day burning Country with the Yunesit'in fire crew in British Columbia, Canada. Photo by Josh Neufeld.

'Until recently, we would have to travel far and wide to find deer. Now they are coming right to us,' one of the ladies said cheerfully, as we walked along.

The Gathering Voices Society arranged for some researchers to monitor the animals and put out field cameras across the areas we were managing. The results were incredible – in the burned areas there were many photos of deer, bears, mountain lions, elk, moose and badgers. It was especially satisfying to have some badgers getting in on the action because they are endangered in British Columbia. These sightings were signs that we were on track to restore the identity of the landscape. It was also reassuring to see that the tree canopies were not scorched by our fire. They looked healthy and green. We always followed the lore of keeping our fires low and cool to protect the trees, so they could live well and grow old.

The next indicator we inspected was the little patches of fresh green grass scattered around the land. This made us very happy because a perfect cultural burn is when the fire does not burn everything and leaves behind a mosaic pattern of black and green. This way resources are still available to the animals and they can continue to make nests and find food after the fire.

As we walked around the area, one of the crew found a chipmunk's nest in the ground where the tiny fellow had bunked in for the winter. We were delighted to see that the den was not harmed at all by the fire and even his trail of chewed-up pinecones was still intact. It was so cute to see the little creature pop his head up out of his den and then quickly duck back underground. Chipmunks are one of my favourite little animals to watch as they run around checking us out.

But it was not only the animals that were showing positive signs of returning; the plants, too, were producing amazing outcomes. The monitoring results gathered by PhD students supporting the fire program showed how the burns led to greater benefits for the food and medicine plants. The Soopolallie bushes, also known as soapberry, are producing five times more berries and have more key nutrients in our burned areas than the plants found in unburned areas. These berries are an important food source for bears, which need them in their diet after hibernation. Further research is exploring how improving the health of the plants through cultural fire will improve the habitat for many other animals.

The next few steps led us to a large patch of Kinnikinnick berries that were alive and well after our burn. We stopped to inspect where the fire had delicately trickled its way between the narrow, fine grass corridors that divided the plants. This was another beautiful example of the right timing, where fire will selectively burn away the dead grass and leave many of the food plants unburned. One of the two camera operators documenting the cultural fire came over to look at the berries.

I was so pleased that this film documentation was happening, recording the Yunesit'in reviving their traditional lands. Everything was going well, and I could see that the fire crew was loving every moment as they grew culturally stronger. It is the same for our communities back home when people go through the process of rebuilding knowledge from Country.

There is still a long way to go, but communities like the Yunesit'in have shown that fire practices can be revived anywhere in the world. From a landscape and people devastated by wildfires, to what we see on Country now is a magical transformation. When we started burning in 2018, the land surrounding the Yunesit'in community was covered in dry grass and dead logs, and we must have burned this land four or five times over in some places. The first time we burned, the fire went right through the entire landscape, burning across all soil types. Like any sick land, this place was highly flammable from being neglected, both before and after the major wildfire event. We had to contain our first fire because it would have kept burning for kilometres due to the area's poor health. But if we did nothing, then the dry grass would build up to trigger another wildfire.

Canada has such a flammable landscape, more so than Australia in some cases. Whether the land is too thick with trees or a guttered mess from wildfire, fire will certainly carry well on neglected landscapes, if given the chance. When we started to work on Yunesit'in Country, we were determined to heal the ravaged landscape from being lifeless and suppressed. The second time we applied fire it was still very hot for the soils because there were thousands of dead, burned trees on the ground.

The safe method is to clean up the logs and burn the heavy fuel loads of grass gradually and gently. In Canada, that also means burning at a time when the soil is wet from the melting snow, so it is protected from the heat generated by the logs that do burn. Some will decay to produce the dust of wood rot; that is when they are ready for a single spark to smoulder into white ash. The landscape will not heal quickly; there is a slow transition back to good health. It needs persistence and vision, with traditional knowledge leading the way.

In Canada, the constant use of land regenerating practices is essential to help the land heal. In other places that have had catastrophic wildfires, such as Hawaii or Los Angeles, the process would be slightly different but carried out with the same dedicated methods. Depending on the climate and terrain, every place has a particular healing strategy that suits it naturally. The urgency is to tend to the affected landscapes before their conditions worsen. These vulnerable areas must not be neglected, or the infernos will happen all over again. Avoiding the responsibility to care for damaged land now will only lengthen the healing process and make the work harder in the future.

The landscape around Yunesit'in is becoming cleaner and the grass is growing thicker where it was once scarce. In the areas we have burned, fir tree seedlings are shooting up naturally, filling the gap where a 1000-year-old Elder tree may have once stood. Frequent fires make the temperature cooler after each burn, which allows for more plant diversity. The weeds become thinner as the landscape receives the regular care it needs to heal.

When I watch the Yunesit'in community burn these areas today, the fire creates the mosaic pattern across the landscape. The flames do not rush off to scorch everything in sight. Instead, the fire trickles along, taking out only what needs to be burned. The fire is starting to behave itself now and it's like a gift to the land instead of a threat that needs to be contained. The people are now burning large areas of land effortlessly and safely, due to the improved health of the landscape, as they build their cultural knowledge.

Teaching children the good fire and controlling it with fir branches in the Tsilhqot'in Nation in British Columbia. Photo by Josh Nuefeld.

The fire is starting to outline the different ecosystems as it goes out around the various soil and tree types that are not ready to burn in that season. It is like unwrapping a big present. This is when you know that the Country is coming back to life and restoring its identity. It is beautiful to watch and soul-nourishing to be a part of the transformation; working with the people from that land to revive it and exercising the connection with Country is the true testament of becoming aligned with nature.

Transforming the health of the land has also created a positive transition for the Yunesit'in community. Before reintroducing the practices of culture burns, all the men could talk about was fighting wildfires or cutting down giant trees for the forest industry. It was a very macho approach. Early on they told me that I was not really a firefighter because I didn't drive a fire truck, wear a fire suit or wield a drip torch and rake. They even said that my fires weren't 'real' fires because they were so small.

'That's not a fire,' one of the men said to me. 'I have lit backburning fires that were 20 metres tall and burned for thousands of hectares.'

I simply replied by saying that was not the right kind of fire for the land.

Over the years that attitude has changed as the men have started to see why cool fires are so important for the land and for them culturally. Now I hear them talk about taking care of the trees and making the land healthy so the animals will return. I've also started to notice that there is much more love and happiness within the group. That alone makes everything we have done so far feel so worthwhile.

The last time I was at the community in 2025, around 30 people wanted to be involved in the traditional burns and to honour their Ancestors. It is a big step up from the small crew we started with and there's every sign that this positive change in attitude will continue to grow stronger. That is the power of reviving culture from Country; it is the magic that can happen here, there and everywhere.

CHAPTER 13

We are water

When I think about water, I go back to my early teenage years swimming in the local river, like most kids from our community did. We would jump off the bridge into the deep rapids and get washed downstream. One day I noticed an older kid sitting on the water's edge staring across to the other side of the river.

He looked at me and said, 'Bet ya I can go underwater and cross to the other side, and come up exactly opposite where we are now.'

I looked at the raging river and told him that it was impossible. But he took in a long, deep breath and slowly disappeared beneath the surface. He was gone for at least a minute and then suddenly he popped up directly opposite me on the other side, as he had promised.

'See, I told you. Now you try,' he shouted, with a smile.

I drew a deep breath and went under the water. Within an instant, I felt the strong current grab hold of me and flush me violently downstream. I recovered and made my way back to the boy, who was laughing at my terrible attempt.

The secret, he said, was to go right down so your belly was flat on the riverbed. At the bottom there is a gentler stream of water where the current is not strong. 'Go down there and crawl along the bottom. Grab onto whatever you can as you go,' he said.

So down I went again, this time with a little more knowledge about the water. I lay flat on my stomach at the bottom of the river, holding onto any rocks I could find to stay on track. I could feel the raging current moving swiftly across my back, trying to rip me from the riverbed and sweep me away. It was hard work, but staying low and hanging onto the rocks kept me moving forward. With a lot of effort, I finally emerged to find myself right on target – straight across on the other side of the river. It was such a good feeling because I didn't think the trick was possible.

I learned something that day and it was more than how to successfully cross whitewater rapids underwater. The river taught me that you could reach your goals in life if you stick to solid foundations. Each one of those rocks on the bottom represented important things to me, like my mentors, family, knowledge and Country.

Stay low, keep close to the earth where everything is safe and calm. Avoid the strong currents that are constantly trying to wash you away from achieving your dreams. That water story helped me structure my life from then on. I knew to avoid people who would try to take advantage of me, and not to let the pressures of life sweep me away.

Like all the natural elements, there is so much to learn from water. The rivers are like the veins of Mother Earth, pumping water continuously around her body. Water is alive, which means it can die if it turns stagnant or is polluted, and then it can no longer support life at all. A dear old friend told me that if water is disturbed it will dry up or run away underground to go somewhere else.

The cycle of water that keeps our planet alive is amazing and there are so many reasons why we need to respect it. Indigenous people have an incredible connection to water and show their respect through the traditional practices of caring for all waterways. I remember back in my younger days walking to a particular lagoon with a special Elder. His Country was made up of wetlands that fed the major rivers running through his homeland. We had to walk a long way through the bush because there was no road to drive there. As we came closer to this natural wonder it began to radiate a very strong presence and it felt as if we were walking into another world.

When the lagoon came into view, I could see that it was huge and I was instantly in awe of its beauty. The water was crystal clear and the lagoon was surrounded by clean sandy banks, where the birds flocked together. Thousands of white waterlilies were dancing in the wind across the surface. The clean white feathers of the magpie geese and the white lilies were so bright they almost blinded me.

As we walked closer, large flocks of ducks and magpie geese took flight in fright and began circling above us. The combined sound of their calls was deafening, and I could no longer hear the grass crunching under our feet as we walked. Soon we couldn't see the sky as thousands of birds flew up in the air, hiding the sun like it was a cloudy day. At that moment, surrounded above and all around by the abundance of life at the lagoon, I knew that there was no better place on Earth to be. It was energising and gratifying.

The Old Man flicked a lure into the water with his fishing rod, and in no time at all he'd hooked a big barramundi for lunch. The fish were plentiful and these lagoons had always been an important food source for Aboriginal people. The Elder then showed me a large flat rock on the edge of the water that had grinding grooves engraved into it. They were used by his Ancestors for crushing lily bulbs and sharpening tools. I stared down at the grooves and then looked around the lagoon, imagining the Old People there enjoying the day: women grinding seeds, people wading through the waters with fish nets, men standing on canoes with spears, kids swimming and collecting mussels. The lagoons are sanctuaries for an abundance of life and they are revitalised every wet season by the gift of floods. So many animals depend on healthy wetlands and Aboriginal people used traditional practices to care for them. Each waterway had its own name, story and lore that helped people to understand how it should be managed.

Most of the lagoons in the Old Man's Country were story places or areas of cultural significance that had been managed for generations. Some were only for men, some just for women, some could not be used for hunting or visited at all, and some were areas where everybody could swim, hunt and dwell with all the families. The lores created different ways of living in relation with the land and waters to ensure these places would thrive. You couldn't help just yourself to any waterhole or place on Country like people selfishly seem to do today.

The Elder explained that in his Country the people did not camp right next to the lagoons because they were special places. The waterholes were left undisturbed to allow the plant and animal life to rest and recover their numbers. You could not go to the toilet or put any human waste in the water because, unlike rivers, most of these lagoons are not running waterways. I understood why this rule was necessary because people gathered plenty of food from these areas. The respect given to these waterways was complex, and there were other lores that applied to different water sources.

Other very important water sources are the cold, sweet and crystal-clear springs that rise from deep underground. They are life-giving in regions where there is not a lot of water on the same level as the ground. For many Aboriginal clans, the springs are story places and hold strong cultural significance. There are spiritual connections with the springs that in some areas relate to newborns and in others are associated with the afterlife. That is another reason why they are treated with great respect.

The main rule I have learned from the Old People about springs is they must never be disturbed in any way. Disturbing a spring by stirring it up, moving rocks around, letting livestock drink from it, or changing its course will pollute the water or lead it to dry up altogether. Some groups have lores about keeping the waters pure, which means you cannot throw food waste or anything foreign into them. Springs must be left alone to ensure that the water continues to rise from deep underground and flows into streams through the land.

For some clans, the lore is that the trees growing around the springs cannot be chopped down, nor can their branches be broken. All the water trees that live alongside rivers, lagoons, beaches and springs play their part in supporting the waterways. They give shade to our rivers and hold the banks together to avoid erosion. They provide habitat for the water creatures and birds. Big river red gums, giant paperbark trees, massive ghost gums, she-oak forests and old coolabah trees are just a few of the many Australian trees that have lived with water forever. Taking care of these trees and understanding their important role is crucial to the future management of our waterways. Most of the waterway ecosystems that these trees live in are sensitive to fire; the fire will stress or kill the trees if the surrounding Country is burned. So, these areas are no-fire Country ecosystems, where the trees and other plants prefer as little burning as possible.

It's necessary to use fire in the right way, so that fire and water support each other. To take care of the water from inland to way out to the sea, good fire management is crucial. That includes burning seasonally to keep the land around the waterways healthy. Well-managed, fire-dependent Country will have good grass cover and strong old trees that stop the topsoil from running off into the river systems.

Elders have told me stories about how clean and full the rivers were in the old times before colonisation. They also said that you could see the gold on the sand at the bottom of the cool running streams. That gold stayed in the water for thousands of years. There was no need to dig it out as it was too soft to be used for tools or anything like that. The Old People left the gold in the rivers to mix with the sand and do the job of purifying the water. Yet the Gold Rush in the nineteenth century in Victoria and elsewhere in Australia and in California in the United States, showed the lengths people would go to in their quest for gold. Today gold is still the most valued resource pulled from the Earth. Having something so highly valued that comes from the natural environment can lead to disaster for our land and waters. Mining gold, coal or any other mineral is a constant threat to the quality of our water. It is a clear example of how the quest for financial profit in the modern age hurts the most precious natural substances on Earth.

While Aboriginal people had no use for gold, there was another resource in the waterways that they did value. I am talking about sand. Sand is an essential part of our environment and it also has many cultural uses and stories. I often think about the time I camped on a massive sandbar along the river with a special Old Man who was my adopted father and mentor. The sand was beautifully white and clean, which made the area an inviting place to stay.

I set up a couple of small tents out in the middle of the sand, a good distance away from the river. We each rolled out a swag and a blanket to keep us warm during the night. Then we decided to go down to the river, to catch a fish or two for dinner. As we walked there, the Old Man spotted the tail of a big sand goanna sticking out of a hole in a sandbank. It was the season for hunting these lizards, and he was keen to catch it and cook it up on the fire. In one smooth action, he pulled the goanna out by the tail, then swung it around and smacked it hard onto the ground, killing it instantly.

He held the limp carcass with one hand, looking it up and down while feeling the lizard's legs and body. 'He is nice and fat, this one, boy,' the Old Man said in a steady voice.

We went back to camp straight away and made a fire to start the lengthy cooking process. First, he skilfully heated up the goanna on the fire and then gutted it. Then he laid the goanna on a flat bed of hot coals, covered it with wet paperback, and buried it in the clean river sand. The little sand oven cooked the lizard beautifully right through.

That night we sat by the fire eating chunks of goanna meat, while I listened to the Old Man's stories. The moon was almost full and before long it was lighting up the area as if it was daylight. I stood up and walked away from the fire to gaze across to the water, with the bright moonbeams shining down and reflecting off the white sandbar.

'This is why the Old People camped on the sand, boy,' the Elder said proudly, while lighting up his pipe. 'You can see everything at night when the moon shines on the sand.' He then pointed out a glowing ring around the moon. 'It's going to be cold tonight, boy,' he said. 'The moon is making a bark hut to keep warm. That's why the ring is around it.'

The Old Man knew many stories about the sky. It is a special part of nature that we sometimes overlook. There has been so much knowledge passed down about the stars that relate to everything we do on the ground. The sky is a holder of stories; it helps us navigate, tells us when to hunt – as it did on that night – and it sometimes tells us to rug up to stay warm.

After finishing his last story, the Old Man got up and walked to his tent to settle down for the night. He lay sideways on his swag, leaving the tent door wide open to let the firelight shine in. He then placed one ear to the sandy ground as if he was listening for something deep under the surface.

'This is how the Old People used to sleep on the sand, boy,' he said. 'This way you can hear anything walking around on the sand while you are sleeping. Crunch, crunch, crunch the sound will go – you can hear someone sneaking up on you from a long way.'

I gave a little chuckle and thought about that last bit of wisdom as I lay down and closed my eyes. After a few hours, I was woken by an early hour chill. I could feel the cool moisture in the air as the dew came down heavily over our tents. The moon wasn't joking about building that bark hut to keep warm, alright. I looked up to see the Old Man huddled in his tent and he seemed to be fast asleep. It was freezing so I pulled the blanket over my head and tried to get as warm as possible for the rest of the night.

At some point I managed to go back to sleep, and in the blink of an eye I woke up and morning was upon us. I looked over to the Old Man's tent but didn't see any sign of him. I called out to him but there was not a sound. I walked over and saw that his blanket was gone but there was no trace of him to be seen anywhere. I called out again in different directions, until I heard the faint murmur of a response.

After another call I could hear the Old Man again, a little louder this time.

'Over here, boy,' he said in a low, muffled voice.

His voice was coming from a bunch of green gum tree branches on the sand. The bunch was no bigger than a regular bunch of flowers. I went over and looked down at the branches, only to see the Old Man's eyes staring back at me through the leaves.

'Morning, boy,' he said in his usual way, as if everything was normal.

He had completely buried himself under the sand to keep warm during the night and the branches were covering his face so he could breathe. The leaves were also a way to stop the mosquitos from buzzing around his face. It was amazing to see him completely buried in the sand and then watching him rise out of it to meet the day.

'Ahh, I had a good sleep, boy, nice and warm under the sand,' he said as he stood up and brushed his clothes down.

Thinking about sand will always bring me good memories of those healthy waterways, but since my first visits to the lagoons with the Old People, things have changed. Thirty years later I went back to check on those special lagoons on their Country and to honour the Old People in spirit, as they had passed by then. When I walked to that beautiful lagoon, there was not a sound to be heard except the slow cry of a crow. The water was a dirty brown and the banks were all muddy, with pig and cow tracks everywhere. There were only handfuls of white waterlilies here and there because the feral pigs, horses and cows had eaten most of them. There were no flocks of birds filling up the skies and blocking out the sun. Instead, three magpie geese were standing by the water looking puzzled. Their feathers were no longer a bright white because the mud had coloured them a gunky brown. I stood on one side of the lagoon and watched wild pigs digging up any remaining source of native life to eat. The sand that used to support the diversity of life in this special place had gone.

Ducks and geese need to eat small amounts of sand to help them digest their food. If we lose the sand then we lose the birds, the fish, the lilies and ultimately, the quality of the water turns bad. Almost a metre of mud and silt covered the lagoon's banks and water basin. The big flat rock with the grinding grooves was buried in sludge and could no longer be seen. It was so sad to see the lagoon in that state, and it made me feel sorry for the Old People and their Country. As I stood there looking at the remote waterhole, it dawned on me that all the great work the Old People did in looking after their Country had fallen away. The scary part was that the Old People had said that the Country would go with them when they died, and it was certainly looking that way.

Right around Australia, lagoons and rivers are slowly filling up with mud and silt from many years of bad land management. The land clearing, overgrazing of livestock, cropping, mining, development and wildfires all contribute to the demise of these waterways. Practising good land and fire management across the continent is only the first step to good water management. We need to ensure that soils are not baked in a way that hardens the ground and decreases its drainage ability. If sand is burned too hot it tends to melt the ground's surface. After all, sand is used to make glass. A hot fire can transform a surface of loose sand into a sandstone crust. This makes the ground less absorbent, so the water is prone to run along the surface in great volume and speed instead of soaking into the ground. That leads to more erosion, which brings different soil types and foreign matter into the waterways.

Making sure that parent trees are healthy and encouraged to return to old-growth forests is another part of caring for water. Trees help protect the land during floods and keep the soil moist in the dry season. Helping the fire-dependent trees to stay healthy in their landscapes is just as important as taking care of the water trees in the flood plains. Clearing the land of trees has had a terrible effect on the rivers and waterways in many countries. Combined with agriculture and mining, this has resulted in river systems being dammed, polluted or drying up. Trees are cleared right down to the riverbanks and often houses or even industrial complexes are built right next to the water. Weeds spread by livestock and through agriculture choke up most waterways in Australia. I have even seen cattle walking through fragile creeks, eroding the banks and leaving their waste floating downstream. In Australia, the contours of the land in some areas show that there were many more wetlands throughout the continent before modern development took its toll.

Another big water issue is the increasing risk of floods. Over generations, Aboriginal people learned that certain landscapes would flood, and they had social practices to avoid dwelling permanently in those areas. That is why they would move to highlands to find shelter and keep dry during the wet season. Modern statistics that go back around 200 years or less might not have recorded any bad floods, so governments and individuals think it is safe to build in an area based on recent history. But just because a flood plain has not flooded in the last 100 years or more doesn't mean it won't happen in the future. If it is a flood plain or lowland area, there's always the risk it will happen. Then, when that land does go under water, it is considered a disastrous, record-breaking event that has never been witnessed before. Regions are devastated, many people suffer, yet a few months later they start building there again. Another decade or many years later it happens again; floods and fires keep occurring.

The threat of flood-related disasters is similar to the threat of wildfires, and just as with wildfires, the general concerns in regions that suffer from floods are mainly about the loss of life and property. The approach to floods and fire is based on response, instead of proactive attempts to prevent them. Floods can be catastrophic, which means that people are now as scared of water as they are of fire. I have seen people panicking when it starts to rain, because they are afraid of being washed away.

Floods are less problematic for nature. The wet season brings life to the land and waterways, the plant and animal populations spike, and the vegetation becomes lush and healthy. The concern is when we don't get major rain and floods in the wet season, as the land needs the clean, revitalising water. We have problems with floods when human dwellings and activity get in the way of the water courses. Nature and humans both suffer when floods wash houses and cars downstream, along with sewage, chemicals and oil spills. They all pollute the water and then run out to sea. Truckloads of plastic bags and rubbish are also washed into the ocean or get tangled in root systems and snags along the riverbanks. Sugarcane and other major agricultural crops leach poisons into the waterways, such as chemicals from crop dusting land in river basin areas. Microparticles of rubber from car tyres that have worn down on the roads are also washed into these systems.

When floodwaters rush through the river basins and out to sea, a plume forms where the freshwater meets the saltwater. That plume needs to be clean and not full of harmful waste products or poisons from humans and industries. The dirty water is equivalent to the massive plumes of black smoke that come from wildfires on the land.

Pollution is filling our seas at a faster rate than ever before, as we see increases in wet-weather events. This affects the health of the outer reefs and adjoining oceans, and if our oceans become lifeless then the land that we depend on does too.

To slow down and even stop this threat, modern society can learn from traditional knowledge and the lores that apply to waterways. Camping away from rivers and waterways is a smart way to avoid human loss and ensure the good health of the land and sea, for example. Yes, you can visit and enjoy these locations, but don't build permanent structures there that can eventually pollute the oceans.

Today, many people want that multimillion-dollar view, so waterside real estate is the most valuable of all. One challenge is to change this attitude and to take practical steps to protect lives, property and nature. Think how good it would be if houses and businesses in high-risk areas were relocated to make way for water restoration. To free some of the rivers and give them back their flood-plain Country, and to encourage the natural habitat to thrive around them. Surely saving billions of dollars from the damage bill would eventually cover the cost of relocating people and businesses away from the flood plains.

Every river should have a buffer of healthy native ecosystems thriving alongside it to keep the water clean and protected. These buffer zones should be at least a few hundred metres to a kilometre wide, depending on the characteristics of the surrounding landscapes. Like any problem that has gone on for far too long, it will take a huge amount of work and money to turn things around, but it needs to be done and it has to start now. Otherwise, the disasters will continue with even greater losses to life and property until people are forced to move anyway.

I once visited an Indigenous community in Central Queensland that used to have a beautiful freshwater river running past their backyards. They could catch fish to feed their families, and the children swam in the river every day. Now a dry, sandy riverbed marks where the water used to flow. The only time there is water in the river is in the wet season. That is all because the big mining companies that work in the area are helping themselves to the water at its source. In Western Australia, I visited another community that had rivers running through their Country. In this case the water flows all year round, but it is nothing but a tease for the people who live there. The children there can't swim in the river because agricultural runoffs have filled it with poisons. The local people can no longer enjoy the simple luxury of going fishing. It is nothing short of criminal for rivers to be treated this way and to leave the people who live near them to struggle with health issues caused by pollution.

Thinking about those places made me realise how fortunate we are in my homelands to be able to drink the water, eat the fish and take a refreshing swim on a hot summer's day. It made me wonder if my children's children will have that same privilege. The government receives many mining and agricultural development applications for our area, and if approved, these developments could harm and even kill our waterways. It is essential that we protect the waterways that are still healthy and revive others, if we can.

Another water story that I find powerful came from my own backyard in Cairns, North Queensland, in Djabugay Country. There is a special waterhole I have been going to for over twenty years and it is a magical oasis. A short walk through lush rainforest takes you to this deep, crystal-clear waterhole that runs into rapids further downstream. It's surrounded by massive trees that shade it and provide branches so you can jump into the water.

When I started visiting the area there were hardly any other people around and it was filled with wildlife. I would take my children there late in the day and we'd quietly walk down to the water to try to spot a platypus. Every time we went there, we would see two or three platypus and we'd watch them paddling around until it got too dark. It was like an untouched paradise, yet it was right next door to the suburbs.

Eventually, as those suburbs grew, the waterhole suffered. Local teenagers decided that it was the perfect party place. On a number of occasions, I went down there to find parties in full swing with loud music blaring. It was disgusting to see the fast-food wrappers everywhere, and plastic and glass bottles thrown on the ground. The teenagers climbed the trees and nailed pieces of wood to them to use as steps and tied ropes around their branches for swings. The constant parties and abuse of the area changed it completely. I noticed the platypus had moved away, perhaps scared off by the noise and all the people.

It was sad to see this beautiful waterhole being treated like a toilet, but a few years passed and something amazing happened. One day we went down there and found that the trees the teenagers would swing off had all fallen into the water. The big logs choked up the waterhole, creating good snags for the fish and river turtles to live in. It made the place feel dark and eerie, as if there was some kind of danger present. Now it was practically impossible for the youngsters to jump off the branches, as they used to do over and over. Although it was not as beautiful as it once was, I was happy to see the place at peace. It had taken enough abuse and now it appeared to have shut itself down to be rid of the noise and mistreatment it had endured. It was quiet there again. The water and the land that supports it were alive and well. The Old People were right when they said the water will react if we mistreat it. If only people would respect these places and understand that our energy has an impact on where we live. Imagine what the world would be like if everyone who uses the waterways was culturally aligned with nature and was curious to learn traditional knowledge.

We have brought cultural fire into mainstream management practices; now we also need to focus on the restoration of the waterways. To clean out the weeds, rubbish and noxious fish. To stop damming the rivers and to allow them to flow. These would be the dream outcomes for many landscapes around the world. To restore the health of a river would be like unclogging one of the Earth's arteries to let the blood flow again. Life will come back wherever water is restored underground, in our rivers, in our oceans, or raining down from the skies. The respectful way to understand water is to acknowledge that it is a living element that plays a key role in our lives and in creation.

We are water.

CHAPTER 14

Indigenous knowledge and agriculture

The Elders told me many stories about the old days of working as stockmen on pastoral properties, when they would ride horses across the land, mustering cattle. My greatest mentors were cattlemen and my uncle was a head stockman in the Gulf Country of North Queensland for most of his life. Generally, the Aboriginal stockmen did not get paid very much, if at all. They usually worked for rations or for a very low wage. They were hard days, but the old stockmen used to talk proudly about their work managing the land for the white station owners and the adventures they had along the way.

Most of those Old People have passed now. They were strong men and women, who worked in tough conditions. The stockmen slept on the ground, even in heavy rains, and rode in the harshest weather, moving cattle across the land for weeks on end. Cattle trucks were not around then so the stockmen on horseback had to take herds to saleyards hundreds of kilometres away. The stories from those earlier times gave me great insights into the ways the stockmen worked the land to sustain a cattle operation.

In northern Australia in the early 1900s, many first-generation farmers relied on Aboriginal stewardship to support their livelihoods. Aboriginal people formed the backbone of the workforce on many properties, using techniques that were not too different from the ways they had maintained the land before colonisation. To muster the cattle and meet the demands of the station owners, they had to cover every hectare of land. With no modern technology or machinery, they relied on traditional knowledge and hard work to do their jobs in the most efficient way. Fire was regularly used to maintain good pastures and to keep the land open and clean. Everyone I've met who was a stockman in those days talked about how open the countryside was, with hectares of native grass.

Today you can't ride a horse through most of those places because it is too thickly overgrown with invasive exotic and native plants. The land is no longer worked the way it used to be. Back then in the northern areas of Australia, they did not clear the land of all the trees. Land clearing was done in many farming regions further south, but in some remote areas in the north the techniques were more in sync with the land. They chopped down lots of trees to build fences and cattle yards but never cleared the area completely.

Although not native to Australia, cattle come from fire-prone landscapes. That is why burning off was an effective mustering practice, as it lured the cattle to areas where it was easier to bring the herd together. Fire offers the same benefits to cattle as it does to kangaroos: the burns produce fresh grass shoots, ready for eating. Wherever there is fire, these animals will follow their noses.

Aboriginal fire management ensures that grass cover is promoted all year round to maintain a good food source. The old stockmen would burn the land at the right time to make sure the grass would shoot back straight away. The wrong timing would leave the land bare for months. Today, many farmers are scared to burn as they have experienced an incorrect application, where the grass did not grow back for a long time. Bare dirt won't feed their cattle, so some farmers believe that leaving the dead grass unburned is better than no grass at all. However, the old dry grass has few nutrients, and many old grasses can be too sharp for grass-eating animals to digest. When the beasts do not touch the old vegetation, it becomes matted on the ground, suppressing the new growth of native plants, and unpalatable weeds start to take over. The landscape can become choked-up and scrubby and wildfires are more likely to occur through the drier times.

The Old Men told me how they burned the land on horseback, riding around targeting the right places to create feeding grounds for cattle. This same practice was used to create good grass for kangaroos and prepare areas for hunting them. When applying fire for the animals this way, the Old People would light up many areas that were scattered around the countryside. This ensured there were safe places for cattle and native animals to go during the hot summer, and that the cattle did not overgraze and flog the regrowth of native grasses in the burned areas. Creating plenty of burn sites also gave the vegetation more time to grow back. By contrast, putting in just one or two burns would bring a concentration of animals to one place, where they would eat out all the new growth.

Indigenous land management is partly based on resting the land, a concept that was implemented in the early cattle days. Lighting the different ecosystems at the right time and managing the frequency of the burns ensured that the fire did not burn the whole property. This also meant that the growth and age of the vegetation varied across the landscape. If some places were green and healthy, they could be left alone to burn another year.

Today, ranchers practise a technique for resting the land that is known as cell grazing, which involves rotating grazing across many paddocks. In some regions it can achieve good pastures without using fire. Many people think it is a new practice, but it has been applied naturally by nomadic peoples for generations. Cell grazing today ensures the land is not over-consumed. Overgrazing, on the other hand, has a devastating impact on the land and for livelihoods. For example, many farmers with overgrazed, poorly managed land experience hardship in times of drought. They have to buy stockfeed or transport their cattle to other pastures. To make things worse, the stress of all this hardens the soils and the grass becomes sparse. Combining Indigenous fire and land management with cell grazing can be beneficial to some modern farming practices. Cattle farmers and others can always learn from the older practices that came from the land to try to improve agriculture today.

Eventually, traditional methods used in Australia by the early stockmen were replaced or abandoned, and the condition of the land in many areas began to deteriorate. That led to a loss of cultural knowledge on the cattle stations. Farmers started to use new technologies to make their work easier, but this often resulted in poorly managed land. Helicopters replaced horses to round up cattle, and bull catchers crashing through the bush became the norm in many places. Without the use of traditional fire, thick weeds and understorey plants flourished and covered the ground. This made the land far less accessible and mustering became more difficult. To overcome this, many farmers started to use spear traps to muster cattle. That usually involves fencing a waterhole and making a one-way entrance of fence rails in the formation of a spearhead. The cattle go in easily enough to drink the water, but find it impossible to get back out.

As well as cattle, pigs and horses also continue to cause major damage to our waterways. The Elders told me that the lagoons and lakes had crystal-clear water before livestock was brought in to graze, and they would catch fish to sustain themselves after a hard day's work. I could see the pain on their faces when they looked at muddy, dried-up ground that was once an oasis. Some lagoons were significant cultural places but that made no difference to many property owners.

Many farmers have cleared the land by using a devastating practice known as chain pulling. This involves attaching a long, thick chain to a huge anchor in the ground and connecting it to the back of a bulldozer. The process is to stretch out the chain and drive circles through native forests, ripping out everything in its path. Then the dead trees are pushed into a big pile and burned. If saplings shoot up, the famers apply a secondary practice known as stick raking, where they knock down the young trees and rake up the sticks to pile burn. This slash-and-burn method clears the land completely, creating massive paddocks of grass to feed large numbers of stock.

The heavy machinery required to clear the trees in this way also damages the soil in many cases. Land clearing is up there as one of the leading causes of environmental degradation and yet it is still used today. In many regions around Australia, chain pulling has left the area in such poor condition that it will take a long time with good management for the land to recover. In some rural areas I've visited, the land is cleared as far as the eye can see – the flat, open ground extending to the distant horizon. Driving across this land for hours without seeing a single tree always makes me feel sick in the stomach.

I have seen paddocks that were totally overgrazed, with the livestock in them eating the dirt off the ground. Hundreds of dead trees lay in some paddocks with raggedy sheep stepping over them in search of a blade of grass. I have also travelled these areas in the middle of the wet season, when the paddocks should be covered in grass. But even after 400 millimetres of rain, there was no grass growing at all in some places. The soils had been run-down for so long that they were no longer fertile. Some of these farms are owned by large companies that are only focused on achieving high profits.

In contrast to these alarming examples, there are also well-managed farms that I have the pleasure of being involved with. I am working with a few station properties through our organisation Living Knowledge Place, and we are exploring ways cattle farmers can benefit from learning traditional fire and land knowledge. All the people involved in this project come from small, family-run properties and they want to improve their practice locally. In most cases they are third- or fourth-generation station owners who inherited their properties and practices from their grandparents and parents. I was heartened when one farmer said that they want to hand the property on to their kids in better condition than the way their parents had left it for them.

A fourth-generation farming family I met in northern Queensland farmed organic cattle, so it was important for them to use natural farming practices that supported the environment. They were a beautiful family and had built a good relationship with the local Traditional Owners. Over a cup of tea, I explained the possibility of a pilot project to introduce Indigenous fire knowledge to improve their livelihood.

The couple who had previously owned the farm accepted that in their old age they should hand the business on to their children and grandchildren to run. The old man told me that they always thought fire was a bad thing for their pastoral business. However, after a long conversation in which I explained the fire process, the family were keen to try out something they had not considered before. They were the only farmers out of the many in the region who'd thrown their hat in the ring. If we could achieve a good outcome with this first project, then perhaps more farmers in the area would follow.

The Traditional Owners were also part of the program, and we walked across the family's property together. We visited areas that had been cleared of trees to create feeding pastures for cattle. Now, thousands of invasive native plants were growing there, choking the land to the point where it was totally unusable. The introduced vegetation was so thick that the land could not support a kangaroo, let alone a cow. But we were determined to improve that land.

We visited a large bloodwood tree and saw that native grass was growing around the base of the trunk, which was a good sign. Then I pointed out another large bloodwood 15 metres away and there were far fewer invasive plants growing between the two big old trees. Instead of woody weeds and leaf litter, native grasses were growing there. When the station owners saw this, they began to understand the role of the parent trees that belonged in that soil type. Those old trees maintain the identity and the diversity of the plants and animals that depend on the system. One of the farmers was struck with excitement and a big smile stretched across his face.

'We need to bring back the parent trees as part of our farming methods, to look after the land in the future,' he said happily. 'It's going to take a while, but we can start the process now.'

I explained that it is possible to bring back the right trees by using precision burning to activate them. Applying the right fire for that type of Country to produce the right heat for the soils is key to that activation. As we continued to walk through the scrubby bushland, we came across areas where a bulldozer had cleared the land. The soils there were still disturbed years later and the grass had not grown back. In the areas where dead trees had been pushed into piles and burned, all that remained was baked soil from the extreme heat covered in thick white ash.

I told the family how Indigenous land management was strictly based on not disturbing the soils. This way, a ground cover of diverse native vegetation could grow, providing food for the animals. The farmer looked at the piles of soil that had been pushed up by the bulldozer blades and nodded.

'I guess we have to use machinery a lot less than what we have been doing,' he said. 'At least now we're learning to keep the land productive through natural ways of using fire.'

We chose the middle of the wet season to put the first fire into the infestation of thick woody scrub. That was the right time because there was plenty of lush green land surrounding the area, which reassured the farmer.

Everyone involved in the project could see the positive results after the first burn. The land started to open up and more native grasses began to grow. Many of the invasive understorey plants had died from the heat and there was little evidence of them shooting back. The young bloodwood trees were not affected by the fire, so they continued to establish their community. The message that stood out for the farmers following the burn was that they didn't have to use any poisons to kill the invasive plants. That was good news, given that there was no place for toxic poisons on their organic cattle property.

One of the farmers looked at the effect of the burn like it was some kind of magic trick. But in fact, it is all about the ways different plants tolerate fire. Every species of plant has its own response to heat, which is one way Mother Nature creates diversity through fire. If all plants responded to the same level of heat in the same way, we would not have ecosystem diversity at all. That is also why Indigenous fire methods are used to burn different vegetation types at specific times of the year. Tens of thousands of years of Aboriginal burning has assisted the plants to evolve and respond this way. That complexity is the reason it takes time to teach fire practitioners how to apply fire depending on the identity of Country.

The next year I returned to the site to burn again, and the following year we all came back to inspect the transformation. We stood on the land we had burned in the summer months during the rainy season. I asked the farmers to light up the land once more as part of a learning experiment, but this time the fire did not catch on at all. Bloodwood Country is traditionally burned in the cooler winter months. The fact that it was not burning in the early summer season showed a shift in the vegetation layer, as the original native grasses were growing back. The time for burning had changed because the sick landscape was recovering and returning to its natural productive state.

I had filmed the process to document our work as a case study and shared it with the project partners. The natural resource management organisation that supported the program used the film to help farmers and presented it at their conferences. We also invited other farmers in the region to a workshop to see the results and experience a burn. A few more graziers turned up and became interested. From there, the momentum began to grow. Before long, we were able to extend the research project across a few regions. I was proud of everyone involved for this achievement, because it's rare for Indigenous knowledge to lead research. As each farmer has their own specific problems to deal with, we are developing a range of case studies to learn and work from.

Most of all, the programs improved relationships between the farmers and the local Indigenous peoples. We are training Traditional Owners to do the work of healing the land and creating jobs in the process. They could become the local land management force that we need. And the farmers involved are happy that the Traditional Owners are there to help with new productive opportunities.

My Uncle Russell is an amazing Aboriginal Elder and his knowledge of the land always proves to be useful for any initiative involving community and Country. He and I visited a property in his area where there was a big lagoon that was an important place for the local Aboriginal people. The Elders had told Uncle Russell about this wonderful place when he was young, but he had never been allowed to go there because it was on private property. Uncle explained that he and other local people couldn't visit many of their significant places because in most cases the gates to the properties were locked and sometimes the farmers would point a gun at them if they tried to go in. Visiting that day, I watched the farmer from this property open the gates and welcome Uncle in with a handshake. The farmer needed help to manage the land and he knew that it may be possible through what we were able to offer.

We drove to the lagoon, and it was exactly as the Elders had described it to Uncle Russell. Now in his seventies, he stood before the massive waterway for the very first time and started pointing at things as if he had been there all his life. He had heard so many stories about the place that he knew where the small rivers entered the lagoon and where the fish were. He even warned me that crocodiles might be in the water due to the rivers that run from there to the saltwater. It was a magical moment to see him visit that place for the first time. There was healing happening right before our eyes and we hadn't even started to talk about how we could improve the land with fire.

Modern science is exploring good alternatives to current farming practices. For example, creating supplements to feed cattle so they produce less methane gas and developing fake meat of all kinds to replace animal products. These innovations are great, but why aren't we also focusing on the obvious solution to so many issues for the agriculture industry: to improve the health of our natural world? Then the environment can thrive alongside industry.

We need to look to traditional knowledge for the answers, or at least give it the chance to demonstrate what's possible. Industries and individuals can draw on this ancient and practical knowledge to find ways to operate efficiently and profitably while also protecting the environment. If we can do that, then the divisions between industry, community and the health of our planet can improve. It can be done. Mother Nature has shown that it is possible, through the work we have done already, to improve agriculture with traditional knowledge. Even more exciting will be the ways the next generations use this knowledge to improve agriculture and encourage a healthy planet into the future.

CHAPTER 15

Respecting people and place

There is a strict social lore among Indigenous communities in Australia where no one is allowed to speak for another person's Country. It is one of the most common lores that is still respected in Aboriginal culture today, where hundreds of nations on one continent acknowledge boundaries and language groups of kinship. Of course, there were wars among tribes to settle disputes, but the identity of people and place was strongly upheld in cultural protocol. In the time before colonisation, if people had not maintained this lore, then all the different clans and languages would not have continued to exist.

Aboriginal people have been on their traditional homelands for countless generations, evolving with the land. Respecting tribal boundaries helped to keep the balance and insured their homelands were not disrupted. Every nation looked after their ancestral landscapes, which allowed for plenty of diversity to exist socially and environmentally.

In the past, every living area evolved to a healthy state and its identity was maintained to ensure that plants and animals thrived. However, if nature's ecosystems are disturbed, their health is affected, and they become unbalanced and vulnerable. This allows plants from other ecosystems to invade, often destroying the biodiversity of the host landscape so it loses its identity. Many plants and animals become a casualty of this change and may even be wiped out altogether. Food for people and animals then becomes scarce, eventually leading to starvation. Only a balanced landscape would support the traditional hunting and gathering lifestyle of Indigenous peoples. Aboriginal land management was perfected to avoid conflicts in nature, while maintaining resilient ecosystems with strong identities and preventing the introduction of invasive plant species. To avoid upsetting the balance, they kept everything in its own Country, where it belonged. In my mind, this is where the mastery of quarantine comes in and it has been used effectively for thousands of years.

The early settlers didn't really understand or practise the knowledge of quarantine. They didn't think about the problems that could arise by introducing plants, animals or people from different parts of the world. In Australia, for example, pigs, foxes, cats, cane toads and a range of exotic plants were brought in, and they have devastated natural resources. This issue has created so much imbalance to landscapes globally and has shaped many of the social and environmental problems we battle with today. It was clever of those people to make guns and steel and develop technology, but the lores of Mother Nature also needed to be respected. This respect is part of the formula that can help restore the land, after all the damage that has been done. It may be hard for many people to understand this today because they live in a social structure disconnected from nature.

The first settlers in Australia classed Aboriginal people as flora and fauna. This offended many people, both Indigenous and non-Indigenous, and is brought up regularly in human rights debates. It did not change until Australians voted in a referendum on 27 May 1967, to amend the Constitution so that Aboriginal and Torres Strait Islander peoples would be counted as part of the population. In the past, there was also the belief that Australia was unoccupied and it was declared *terra nullius* (land belonging to no one).

Until the Mabo Case when the High Court of Australia ruled in June 1992 that Aboriginal people had held native title to the land prior to colonisation in 1788, Indigenous people were accused of not occupying the land at all. That is far from the truth, as we know, just as being classified as non-human is a terrible insult. But on the other hand, being declared as flora and fauna is sort of cool, if you really think about it – even though the colonisers would not have meant it as a compliment. Basically, it was saying that the people are nature and acknowledged that they are part of the landscape.

In my mind, the Indigenous people of any continent should be considered as part of their natural environment. It is the first social layer to respectfully consider when looking for positive ways forward in a changing world. These people have inherited knowledge and customs tied to the ancestral lands that they are responsible for. There is no separation between the original peoples and nature, as they are both needed to restore each other.

If the land dies, then the people will die with it; if the land heals, then the people will heal with it.

Historically, the first settlers of the Australian towns were made up of many nationalities. Although their descendants are not indigenous to those areas, most are now born in the towns and rightfully consider them their home. In some places the non-Indigenous community get along well with the Indigenous people, but that is not always the case. I find it easier to achieve good collaborative restoration programs in places where people get along. When the Traditional Owners invite us and the non-Indigenous community is in full support, then we are likely to achieve constructive outcomes. Working respectfully together establishes pathways for a strong, resilient community. I have also worked in many regions where there is bigotry within the general community. Often when I go to fractured places like that, I discover that the land is in a devastated state of health. In every case, finding ways to get people to work together is fundamental to healing people and place.

The job of healing the land is massive and not one group or individual can do it alone. Everybody in each region has their part to play to achieve what Country requires of us, and that is to make nature our priority. Every individual in the community needs to respect place in a way that improves the social structure in that area. Nothing can go forward without considering the interests of all neighbours and local stakeholders within any district. From my experience, the best way to make this happen is to use Indigenous solutions, which benefit everyone. This is simply a case of working from the ground up until we all reach the sky.

Let's follow the story of a tree growing to an old age in its native place. That tree benefits everything in its Country through the design of nature. It enriches the soil to keep it healthy and productive. Many grasses and plants need the tree to be there in order for them to grow. The birds make nests in its branches, and some animals will live in the hollow trunk. The tree's fruits, flowers and seeds create a diverse food source for many species. It cleans the air, its canopy creates shade and the cool breeze blows through its leaves. The tree benefits everything in the natural world and is a clever, interconnected design created by Mother Nature herself.

Indigenous fire practices have evolved to align with the same structure of benefiting Country and Mother Nature. Cultural burning ensures the fire is kept cool, so it does not bake the soil to destroy the organic matter; the tree canopies are not scorched, so their flowering season is not affected. A rich diversity of vegetation reshoots to provide food for the animals. The white grass smoke is gentle on the native bees nesting in the trees, as it dissipates into the air. The art of Aboriginal fire management is but one practice that has been crafted to help the environment thrive and support human occupation at the same time.

Implementing Mother Nature's design into the norms of our modern society is key to aligning more closely to nature and Country. I have seen the broader community benefit after experiencing Indigenous practices that were brought into mainstream solutions. As one example, Aboriginal fire management can help us take better care of our natural environment by improving conservation methods and it can create broad opportunities through a shared culture. Like the tree, the benefits will branch out into many fields of our society – for example, by reducing the threat of wildfires, restoring grasslands, opening up Country and making landscapes more productive to support livelihoods.

Fire practices could also strengthen our economies by encouraging innovation, lower insurance costs by keeping communities safer from wildfire, improve the health of communities by connecting us more with nature, create new jobs and industries related to caring for the environment, and enrich our children's education. Most importantly, traditional fire practices strengthen culture and improve the quality of life. There can be a brighter future if regions and communities recognise these social developments based on the physics of Mother Nature. How we redesign all human practices connected to the wellbeing of everything socially and environmentally is where innovation should lie.

The issue of loss of identity of culture and landscapes is shared across many countries. Case studies of traditional land management practices from around the world could be used to strengthen the concept of respecting people and place globally. Reviving cultural burning practices in the United States and Canada, as I discussed in earlier chapters, reveals the same concepts as Aboriginal fire management in Australia. Many other countries are striving to reclaim their cultural relationships with the land, as they also had similar traditional practices.

Respecting people and place on a global scale can help restore biodiversity while improving human relations at the same time. Acknowledging cultural differences and similarities can lead people around the world to have this respect for each other. Every person on the planet, regardless of where they live, should know their ancestry bloodlines and where their traditions of living with nature existed before many of those traditions were lost. This knowledge has the potential to strengthen the broader shared culture and enhance opportunities for positive change. I've had conversations with people in Italy, Japan and the United States, where they have told me that their Ancestors had traditional fire practices and now they want to revive them.

If people and place are not respected, we will see problems that will fester over time. In many cases, division will occur within a society, and with no process of reconciliation there will be ongoing, intergenerational unrest. There is an example of this in Australia, where people are divided about the date of the country's national day. By 1935, all states in Australia had adopted 26 January as the date for Australia Day – the date in 1788 when the British flag was first raised at Warrane (Sydney Cove), formally establishing the colony of New South Wales, on unceded Aboriginal land. In 1994, 'Australia Day' was officially declared a national annual holiday. Many Indigenous and non-Indigenous people now refer to 26 January as 'Survival Day' or 'Invasion Day' and want to change the date to one that does not commemorate the arrival of the British invaders to this continent. But the Australian Government will not listen to their request or acknowledge the reasons why the date should change.

The argument has been growing stronger, but any resolution seems unlikely in the near future from either side of the fence. It is possible to find a date that celebrates the diversity of the Australian population without 'celebrating' the colonisation of the Aboriginal people and the dispossession of their land. But loud protests to keep the date continue. They are fuelling more hatred and racism from both sides, which disadvantage the entire nation now and into the future.

However, the issue goes much deeper than simply changing a date, which seems like a small task. Aboriginal customs, lores and connection to their traditional lands are constantly ignored or denied. Sacred places are often disrespected and trampled on by people who just want to have a good time in their four-wheel drives. Aboriginal knowledge struggles to be included in the education system. Cultural fire knowledge is not considered as a mainstream solution to wildfires. The list goes on. Over time, this refusal to acknowledge and listen to Aboriginal people has created distrust, humiliation, destroyed confidence and led to a divided nation. Indigenous people and place have hardly been respected since colonisation, and that is why we see a deprived country rather than one that is unified and thriving. There is very little recognition of the reality and impact of the problems faced by Aboriginal people in the past and still today.

Not showing respect to people and place can lead to disengagement and disorganisation. We are seeing this happen around the world. Maybe there would be less disadvantage if people could thrive within their own territories. We need to look at what causes imbalances in the world and do what we can to address them in a proactive way that restores identity and respects diversity.

The Old People would tell me stories about the lores of controlling the population in the past. The balance between the number of people and the natural landscape needed to be in sync. My greatest mentor told me that a man could not father a child unless he had passed initiation into manhood. That was partly so the man had the knowledge to educate his child; then the child could grow up with the right teachings to uphold the lores of people and place, and to become an Elder in the future. This important social structure helped to keep the clan nations strong.

Across the globe, through all the histories of war and colonisation, the actions of the conquerors have disregarded nature's lore and disrespected the people's knowledge and relationship with place. When Indigenous people go to another nation's land, they are visitors to that Country. When colonisers go to another land, they demand their own rights, bring their own beliefs and take ownership of what is not theirs. Environmental decline is the consequence of this past and present trend, because colonisers disregard the fact that people and place are one. People can live outside of their cultural lands as long as they adopt a respect for the Country and culture they are fortunate to reside on.

No matter if you are born on a land that is not your place of cultural origin or have just recently arrived, respect is paramount. It contributes to the ways we create a healthy broader culture that we can all share. Inclusiveness is the key, restoring identity is crucial; caring for each other and applying love is how we activate the healing process. It starts with realigning our practice to the ancient lores of respecting people and place.

CHAPTER 16

It all starts in the stomach

An opportunity came up once for me to work with a group of young adults from an Indigenous community in southern Queensland. We did a cultural burn on one of their properties and it went really well. I visited again a year later to run another workshop with them and to see how the land had responded. Before that burn, the ground had been covered with leaf litter and the weed lantana was choking up the landscape. When we went there again twelve months after the fire, we were greeted with a much healthier forest of diverse grasses, native bush foods and medicine plants. The eager young people were very interested to see this change.

We walked across the area, visiting each little native plant that had shot up after the burn and I told the group about them. 'This plant is a native cherry tree,' I said, while picking the fruits for the young people to try. Then we found a few rosella plants and they learned how to use the leaves in a salad. Everyone was able to feel, smell and taste many of the plants growing there. After an hour of walking and talking, the group was amazed by the diverse range of food plants that had returned to the area.

'I didn't realise our Ancestors ate so many different types of plants,' one young man said.

I explained that people ate what was growing in their Country, and they had thousands of different traditional uses for the plants. This knowledge of food and medicine plants tells us that the diet for Aboriginal people included many plants and was not just meat. Realising that their Ancestors ate these foods made the young people think about their own diet and wellbeing, so they listened with even more interest.

I pointed far across the land and said, 'I want everyone to look around the bush and see if you can find what I am asking for. Can you see any milk or dairy out there on the land?'

'No,' they all responded confidently.

'Well, if you can't see any cow's milk on the land then maybe it is not a good idea to eat too much dairy. I don't think your Ancestors walked around drinking cow's milk and eating cheeses all day.'

They laughed and nodded in agreement.

Next I asked, 'Can you see any wheat growing naturally out there on the land?'

'No,' they said again.

I went on to tell them that wheat didn't grow there. Traditional flours are made from native seeds, bulbs and legumes, which are all gluten free. So too much gluten and modern wheat breads are not that good for you either. Whether it is white or brown wheat bread, it doesn't really make much difference.

Then I asked, 'What about meat? Do you see any sources of meat out there that your Ancestors ate?'

Of course, they knew the answer to that question. All sorts of proteins, such as kangaroo, possum and fish, were available in season. We discussed how traditional meats were much leaner and healthier than the meat that comes from farmed animals that people eat today. Many animals that our Ancestors ate lived on native grasses, fruits, flowers and insects, while most farmed stock are fed on cultivated grains. Some even live in pens away from any native grasses. The Ancestors would spend a day or more hunting for meat, working hard to catch it. Then they would clean it and carry it back to camp. This all involved a lot of physical exercise, which helped the body to digest the meat. Now people consume large amounts of meat without doing any exercise and it can sit in their guts for days. The Old People told me that when they eat meat it has to be cooked rare, so they get all the nutrients from it. Overcooking meat takes away the goodness and will not make you as strong.

There are many amazing Australian saltwater and freshwater foods too. When they are in season, waterlilies and seaweed, fish, mussels, crabs, yabbies and the other beautiful foods are part of the traditional cuisine for the river and coastal peoples.

When I asked the group if they could find eggs in the land, everyone rushed to answer. There are eggs harvested from ducks, geese, turtles and crocodiles, and the list goes on. So, we all agreed that eggs are a part of our traditional diet. Today, we can buy eggs from the supermarket and we should choose ones from free-range or grass-fed chickens. It is even better to eat fresh eggs from your own chickens.

I asked another question. 'Do you see any rice on the land?'

There was a pause for a moment as they were not sure. Wild rice is found on our Country, but people don't usually know that because it is seasonal and many waterways have been so damaged that they can no longer support wild rice. Wild rice is found in many countries and is part of the traditional diet for many Indigenous people around the world.

Then I asked if they could see any fruit out on the land. Of course, they answered, 'Yes.' Plenty of native fruits grow on the land but all our native fruits are small, not like the large fruit available in the shops. The common bigger fruits we know today can contain high levels of sugar and should not be eaten in large amounts. Our small native fruits have less sugar and high levels of vitamins and minerals. In the old times, everything was eaten in season and that is nature's way; seasonal food is very fresh and full of nutrients.

I went on to explain that many of our plant foods and medicines are bitter and even sweet berries have a hint of bitterness. A bitter taste is a feature of the healthy foods and medicines in our traditional diets. Today, many Aboriginal people eat lots of sugary, sweet food, which can lead to health problems. Their tastes have changed and they do not like anything that is bitter. I broke off some leaves from a bitter-tasting medicine plant and gave them to the group to chew on. When I was young, I used to do this all the time, to train myself to enjoy the bitterness so I could eat healthy bitter bush foods.

I asked if there was a cup of tea out there in the bush and the answer again was, 'Yes.' There is a wide range of bush teas, many that are highly nutritious. Some have medicinal properties and, to my knowledge, our traditional teas do not contain caffeine.

Another point I made was that most of our traditional foods are not as acidic as tomatoes and other plant foods from the nightshade family that are sold in supermarkets. Acidic food can cause inflammation like gout so we should not eat too much of it.

I asked them if they could see any fried foods out there cooked in hot oils.

'No,' they all said and there were a few giggles.

No one deep-fried their goanna or made hot chips in the old times. Eating food deep-fried in saturated fats is very popular today but it can lead to obesity and poor health. The Ancestors in Australia and across the globe did use oils but they were extracted naturally from plants and animals. In Australia we collected oils from goannas and emus before or after they were cooked. Other cultures extracted coconut oils and essences from plants. These oils were used in cooking and sometimes for medicinal or spiritual uses.

Next I asked the group how food was cooked traditionally for tens of thousands of years, and many said, 'They cooked on hot coals,' which is always the most common answer, and it is correct. Large shells or wooden coolamons were used for boiling water and soups. The Old People also dug into the ground to make ovens, to bake fish or yams, for example. The equivalent healthy ways to cook today are on a grill or roasting food in a conventional oven. It is also good to cook in pots to make wholesome stews. Many Elders I have known would boast about the goodness of the soups made from plants and animals, and they regarded them as medicinal foods. Traditionally, some plants were prepared by soaking them in cold water for a while, often to draw out their natural poisons before eating them. Raw foods were also very common in the traditional diet.

The group was keen to explore the subject more and it was inspiring to see them taking everything in.

'All this talk about food is making me hungry,' I said with a chuckle. So we walked back to our cars to collect the lunches we'd each packed that morning.

While everyone was sitting around eating and having a laugh, I noticed that a few young men were missing from the group. 'Hey, where did them other fellas go?' I asked everyone.

They all shrugged and turned back to their food. I walked around and found the guys sitting behind a car that was parked away from the others.

I snuck up to surprise them and they all froze, looking up at me with mouths full of greasy fried chicken. They were embarrassed because we'd just had the long discussion about traditional food.

'Aha!' I said with a smile. To avoid making them feel bad I told them it was okay and there was no need to hide.

After lunch I pointed to the peak of a small mountain and told the group that we were going to walk up there. At the top we would discuss how we would do the burn so the fire would trickle down. Most people followed me up the steep hill, but a couple powered ahead like it was a race, which was normal behaviour for those fit young men.

Halfway up I turned to see the boys who'd eaten the fried chicken sitting down on the track, taking a rest from the steep climb. I went back to encourage them to keep walking but found them panting heavily. They were big boys and what alarmed me the most was that they were only eighteen to twenty years old. They should be scooting up that hill leaving me behind, as I was more than twice their age.

'See, it's the fast food that's making you like that,' I said jokingly. Again, I didn't want them to feel embarrassed, so I gave them some encouragement. 'Come on, let's work it off.'

The boys gave a sigh and continued the climb.

The next day we all returned to the land to continue the workshop. This time when lunch came around, everyone, including the boys, brought out healthier food with a good dose of salad in the mix. It was great to see that the boys had changed their diets so quickly, and they didn't hide their lunch this time. Instead, they sat with the group, making sure we noticed what they were eating, which made me smile inside with pride.

The traditional knowledge of food had sunk in with the young people because we'd discussed it in a way that showed how it was an important part of their ancestral identity. By eating foods that matched our traditional diets in the closest possible ways, they were practising their culture. We have all heard the Western medical advice about what foods to eat and to avoid, but it often goes in one ear and out the other. This time the young people heard it in a way that linked them to their land and ancestral knowledge, and that inspired them to commit to a healthier way of living within their culture.

I have shared this knowledge with people I've met in various Indigenous communities over a few years now, and as a result, many of them have also changed their diets. I would return to these communities months later to find the people looking healthy and slim. Their eyes looked brighter, and they seemed much happier than when I first met them. It makes me feel so good when I see people's health improve by connecting to the land through their stomachs.

'Look at you,' I would say. 'You look amazing.'

One person replied with pride, 'I only did what you taught me.' And then gave me the biggest smile.

It is a workshop that I'd love to share more widely, just like the fire workshops that we have successfully held in various places over the years. I have trialled it with a number of Indigenous and non-Indigenous people and I know that it helps to improve their lives. It is important for people from all cultures to think about the food we eat. Also, people can practise their culture when they eat and that is a powerful way to nourish the spirit. It is the foundation to strengthening all aspects of cultural practice, awareness and spirituality. There is so much to learn from the Old People about traditional food lores. For example, there are lores about how plants and animals are harvested, how they thrive with good land management, and which foods are available in each season. The Old People taught me to eat what our land produces and not to eat what does not exist in a natural form.

I know what you're thinking: How do you eat traditionally when you don't have access to traditional foods?

You can find other foods that align with our own. You can eat chicken eggs instead of eggs from native ducks. Choose chickpea or tapioca flour if you can't use flour made from traditional seeds and grains. This way you avoid the effects of gluten and the flour has similar nutritional properties. Strawberries, blueberries, raspberries and other small fruits are similar to our traditional fruits in Australia, and they are packed with minerals and vitamins.

We are led to believe that eating healthy foods is expensive, and it is if you follow commercial programs, but it doesn't have to be. You don't have to shop at expensive health food stores and eat the 'super foods' advertised everywhere. It is not about eating that stuff, it is about what not to eat. Simply take out the foods you shouldn't be eating and live on the staples that are good for you. Many people choose food by price. This can lead them to make poor choices, often out of necessity and without realising that the food might be bad for them. The fact that processed foods are often so cheap is one of the evils of the world.

Drink water, teas or coconut milk instead of soda or energy drinks, and don't be fooled by sugar-free drinks as they are not healthy alternatives. One time in a small community I was driving with an Old Man I had just met and we pulled up at a shop. He wanted to get a drink, and when I asked him what kind, he said that he wanted the healthy soda.

'What healthy soda?' I asked.

'You know, the healthy one,' he said again.

'Which one?' I asked again.

'The cola zero-sugar one,' he said.

I said to him with a chuckle that it was not healthy at all. The zero-sugar soda has no nutritional value and the artificial sweeteners are not exactly a healthy alternative.

Learning about the traditional food lores will help people of all ages understand what they should eat and when. Occasionally the Old People would come with me to the city and we'd go out for dinner. There were times when I would order a dish for them and they would turn it down, saying that they couldn't eat that food. When I asked why, the Elders would simply say that it would make them feel 'No good.' Foods that were bad for their health were also bad for their spirit. They did not want to pollute their spirit or go against their cultural ways. Don't eat too much and don't eat what you shouldn't put into your body if you want physical and spiritual health. Eating the right way makes our spirit pure and that enables us to connect with the spiritual world more strongly. This not only gives good health but can also bring us towards a stronger state of consciousness, so we can think more clearly.

Although my Elders and mentors taught me about the food lores, it took me a long time to realise that I should follow their advice. In my younger days I would eat anything and by the time I turned 40, I was overweight. That was way too young to feel like a blob and experience aching pains in my joints. I felt shameful and disappointed for letting myself go. I thought: What am I doing? I am a cultural practitioner and I have received this wealth of knowledge, but I am not putting it into action.

That's when I decided to change my diet to follow the traditional food lores. It was the easiest dietary shift I have ever made. The weight started to fall off and the pains in my knees went away. My head felt clear and I was much happier. My spirit became strong and I felt more connected to Country and active again. My diet is now more culturally aligned with the natural world, which is a part of me and part of my Ancestors from both sides of my family. I try to choose foods that are similar to the traditional cuisine. For example, I'll have fish with salad but hold the tomatoes and no chips, please. Ditching the chips is really about avoiding the deep-fry cooking process. If I want chips, I bake them in the oven and use sweet potatoes, which are more like traditional yams.

After avoiding these foods for a while, I found that I was a lot less hungry. Back when I was consuming the bad foods, I wanted to eat all the time and could not go without a meal. Eating bad foods is similar to taking drugs or drinking alcohol – it can become addictive. The chemicals in them will make you want to eat even when you are not hungry. Once I stopped eating the addictive foods, I found that I could go for longer between meals. I soon stopped following the routine of breakfast, lunch and dinner, which is drummed into us by the modern world. I let my body fast by skipping a meal or two and only ate when I was hungry. This felt so much more natural than eating when we are expected to. Having long periods between meals was common for the Old People and that is how it can be for us too. If everyone in the world ate like this, we would ease so much pressure on the natural world and perhaps live longer. The paleo diet is also based partly on the foods our Ancestors ate.

What we eat can connect us to culture and our planet through our stomachs. When I share Aboriginal food lore, I also talk to people about the ways our food connects us to Country and how we can choose diets that are influenced by culture.

In my life day to day, I try to match the exercises I do to the physical lifestyle of hunting and gathering, and keep moving as much as possible. Staying active is a big part of honouring the food I am eating. This includes doing the work on Country, the harvesting, climbing hills and healing landscapes with fire.

When I was younger, there were many more Elders in the communities, and they often lived into their eighties and nineties. Now when I visit many communities, there are fewer Elders and they are between 50 and 70 years of age. There's a big difference between the life expectancy for Indigenous people compared with non-Indigenous Australians, and that is no secret. Old photographs of the First Peoples globally showed that many had athletic bodies, with lean physiques and six-packs on the men. So many people are overweight now and that can lead to a range of chronic diseases such as diabetes, which are causing epidemics.

From time to time, it is alright to eat a little of what is not good for us, but indulging every day will only become problematic. If you're at a birthday party, have a slice of cake, especially if a family member made it. Lighten up and live a little. But soon after that, go back to the diet of Country. Sometimes not eating someone's food can be considered rude, so when I am visiting a community I will try to find something that I can eat and enjoy with my hosts.

Food is such an important topic because it has so much to do with the wellbeing of our world, socially and environmentally. For many Indigenous people, the wrong diet is tied to the disadvantage that affects various aspects of their lives. Community shops sell a range of fried foods and their fridges are stacked with coloured sugary drinks. Also, the mindset of what food is culturally has shifted. Tinned meat such as bully beef and spam and devon sausage are almost considered to be cultural food. That's due to the food rations that were handed out to Indigenous workers instead of wages in the hardship days following colonisation in Australia. Many Indigenous people across the world share the same experience, where introduced foods have come to be regarded as part of their cultural diets, even though these foods are not aligned with their traditional practices. In Australia, we have bread called damper, which is made from white flour, salt, milk powder and water and people in the Torres Straits have fried scones made from these same ingredients and fried in seed oils. In America, they have a similar fried bread, and Indigenous people in Canada make a fried bread called bannock.

These breads are examples of foods that are now accepted culturally yet they can contribute to health conditions. In the broader community, non-Indigenous people eat breads manufactured in factories from processed ingredients, which are not aligned with their ancestral diets either.

Indigenous people worldwide have been making traditional breads from tubers, seeds, nuts and grains for thousands of years. Finding ways to introduce versions of foods that are more aligned with our ancestral backgrounds is not only exciting but healthier. There are so many rewards in aligning our diets to culture and nature; the best one – other than improved health – is enhanced taste. Foods taste better because they are made from natural ingredients rather than processed sugars and fats. They have the flavours of the healthy ingredients we should be eating.

Today, chemicals and poisons in foods are slowly sickening people in large numbers. A poor diet can have an impact on the way we think, make us feel tired, and change our moods, making some people irritable and even angry. What we eat can directly affect us as a society, too, and that can be reflected in our ability to work together and open our minds to new ways. If we are going to heal the planet, we need to eat the right foods so we can work hard, think clearly and be happy and healthy.

But how can this happen when food today is often not aligned with our environment and its production is controlled by corporate giants? Small businesses, such as fruit and vegetable shops and food stalls at markets, feel the pressure of corporate competitiveness and many have to close down because of this. It is timely to educate people about our food security and what we can do to better support our communities and planet.

While living off the land like our Ancestors did is not realistic for most people these days, we can still apply some of the traditional practices when it comes to choosing and preparing food. Growing our own foods, even just some plants in small pots, and setting up community markets and cooperative grocery stores are some ideas to consider.

Finding ways to restore happiness, health and identity through our stomachs contributes to restoring the health of our planet and society. We need sustainable food options that are good for the land, rivers and seas. The massive amounts of land clearing done to create farms for livestock is detrimental to our environment. The poisons that are used for crops such as wheat and sugarcane are killing our soils and polluting our rivers. Cotton farming is putting our rivers under stress. Fishing trawlers are ripping the bottom of the ocean with massive nets that capture everything in their path.

It is important that we make the right food choices and think clearly from our stomachs – because so much harm done to Mother Nature is the consequence of what we are doing to ourselves. If we are unhealthy then the land will be unhealthy. That combination will not strengthen our culture or prepare us for the inevitable challenges we will face in the future. Mother Nature needs us to be healthy in every way to take humanity to the next level of intelligence, which is where the ultimate happiness awaits us. Food lore is an extremely important part of that outcome. Teaching our children this is crucial to support the healing era that is upon us today and will be for many generations to come. It all starts in the stomach.

CHAPTER 17

Adaptation

There is no doubt that climate change raises grave concerns for our planet's future, and it is fuelling the call for humanity to change their ways. As I wrote in Chapter 1, many people believe it is real, while others refuse to accept that climate change is happening at all. It appears that those on the political left are extremely concerned about it, while many on the right refer to it as a hoax. This is an unproductive stalemate that doesn't help us find solutions.

Some politicians ignore the facts coming from their own Western scientists. They want to ramp up production in the fossil fuel industry and support companies that are extracting resources from the ground. Meanwhile, politicians and others on the left will do whatever they can to switch to renewable energy and push carbon programs, sometimes regardless of the consequences. Western approaches to dealing with climate change – including those on both the left and the right – do not consider the Indigenous perspective that sees humans as a part of nature. Modern society acts on the belief that people are more important than nature. It seems that protecting lifestyles and political agendas is far more valuable than worrying about the planet – our home.

Many people are confused and misled by the arguments that come from both the left and right sides of politics, which are often tied to money, ego and power. When you add them all up it equals greed. Climate change can be very profitable in a world that is fearful and desperate for a solution. Many countries are relying on initiatives that have not been fully considered or tested; these are sometimes quick fixes that seem to be the right solution at that moment, while traditional knowledge solutions from Indigenous cultures around the world struggle to be heard.

Carbon is a key issue of concern. Companies can buy carbon credits to offset the damage they are doing in another place. This practice seems to be more about accounting than achieving positive long-term outcomes. The carbon-credits market is all about the numbers, and although some funds do trickle down to communities that are working on practical programs, there is plenty of room for improvement.

I don't understand how various carbon programs have different standards when it comes to reducing emissions. Why do some programs invest in one landscape over another? The whole world is precious and the environment in every country needs equal care and support. Otherwise, we can't restore biodiversity and help nature to heal. I have seen landscapes that desperately need the restoration of good fire management and regeneration work and yet they do not qualify for any financial assistance.

There are cases where carbon assessments are done on massive areas of land, where the bushland stretches on for thousands of hectares with beautiful rivers and springs. These places suffer badly from wildfires, but the carbon assessments recommend very little investment based on the type of land and its trees. In one assessment, the suggested financial support wouldn't cover the cost of a vehicle, let alone a full-time position for a fire practitioner.

Many of the programs that I am familiar with favour planting eucalypt trees because they grow faster than some other species. But restoring the right native trees and grasses to the ecosystem is the ultimate solution. For example, many places need to encourage the regrowth of local native grasses, because they play an extremely important role in supporting biodiversity and carbon.

We applied for a carbon program for the Kuku-Thaypan Elders when I was working closely with them on their Country in Cape York Peninsula in Queensland. For years, we burned their land the old way with just knowledge; there was no budget for wages, equipment or anything else. The Old People had been burning their land with cultural fire to keep the wildfires away and to build a career pathway for their families as fire practitioners. Unfortunately, the carbon assessment found that their land did not qualify because it had no recent history of wildfires. We were disappointed because by reviving and using traditional fire practices on their land, we had prevented wildfires and that made them ineligible for financial support.

How can anyone put a higher value on some ecosystems than others, instead of valuing them all equally? Western systems often seem to compartmentalise things. In the end, much of the land misses out, as do the people in those regions. We need to deal with climate change in a holistic, interconnected way. That is essential because living things, including humans, depend on each other to exist and thrive. That is the lore of nature. Everyone needs to step on board to deal with the issues that come with climate change.

So often climate change is seen through a cloud of doom and gloom; we live with the fear that it could wipe us off the planet. It is an especially grave concern for young people, and so it should be because they are the future. I certainly don't want my children's children to inherit a world of chaos that has barely any life left in it.

If we look at human-induced climate change through the Indigenous lens, the problems go way back to when First Peoples were removed from the land. From the time when people were a part of nature, to now being more like parasites, taking the life from the Earth. Even when I was in my late teens, my mentors were ringing the alarm bells about the potential destruction of our world; that was long before the words 'climate change' came into our regular conversations.

The issue of human-induced climate change is modern humanity's way of blaming nature for all the hurt that has been done to our planet. Instead, it is human disconnection from Mother Nature that has caused the damage and created the situation we are in today. All along the way there have been road signs telling people that the Earth is not happy with the way they are treating her. The floods, the wildfires, the massive storms, the extinction of many plants and animals, the air pollution and the toxic waterways are only some of these signs.

Also, let's not forget the constant warnings from Indigenous peoples around the world, which have been ignored for far too long. So many of these people have voiced the need to respect the planet. The cry to stop the greed of modern humanity and the harm it is doing people and our natural world, comes from Indigenous people everywhere. After these warnings failed to drive modern civilization to take notice, the big boss has finally stepped in.

That big boss is the Sun, and it is pretty much the end of the line when the Sun steps in. There are no other warnings after that. Mother Nature has been patient and forgiving for too long. Whether you believe in climate change or not, it does not matter because life on Earth is in danger regardless.

It has taken hundreds of years for the damage being done to the planet to creep up on us. Now we are at the stage where we cannot continue the harmful practices that will destroy our planet. Thinking about the passing of time leads us to the question that so many people ask about climate change: Is it too late to turn things around?

If you look at the way we live in our modern industrial age, then the answer can seem uncertain and perhaps pessimistic. But if we reconnect with our ancestral roots and align with the knowledge of Mother Nature, there is plenty of room for hope. To do that we must understand that transitioning from fossil fuels to clean energy is only the start of the action. So much needs to be done at the corporate level, but how do we make big companies acknowledge their responsibility to care for the planet? Many corporations are the cause of serious damage to our natural world, yet it seems unlikely they will change their practices when they are addicted to corruption and greed. All I hope for is that some of them hear the plea coming from the community level to restore our planet.

We also need a complete shift at that community level, which means educating people about the many ways they can each contribute to healing the planet. Individuals everywhere need to make sacrifices they may not be used to, and for many that will certainly infringe on their privileged world. Getting rid of all plastics, changing food laws to prevent waste, using more public transport or riding bikes, are only a fraction of the things we can do to make a difference.

But that is still not enough; we can go even deeper. There is far more that we need to change to reduce the impact of the capitalist system on our natural world. Many people are spoiled by the unlimited choices of products that are taking too much from the planet. For example, we can eat less seafood for a while and give the oceans a chance to recover. While we are at it, we can introduce ways to harvest seafood sustainably without raping the seas.

When Covid shut the world down, we witnessed the ways nature started to recover from over-consumption by humanity. The water and air quality around the planet improved and the animal population increased, all because humans unintentionally gave the world a rest. We can change our ways to make a huge difference, but that is easier said than done. Many people aren't prepared to change or to give anything up. This is shown clearly in the climate change debate when world leaders can't see past their own agendas. There has to be a turning point, where we put our hands in the dirt and begin the intergenerational era of healing the planet and ourselves.

In times of natural disasters in Australia, making better evacuation plans and improving emergency strategies are certainly needed, but it is far more constructive to apply a proactive approach. We should start to put Country first for a change and focus on healing the land as the highest priority. Doing so will move us away from being a reactive, disaster-and-response society. By being proactive we are investing in everything that exists around us, which is how we ultimately invest in ourselves. People need to gain the ability and skills to understand the land the way our Ancestors did for so long.

The natural process of climate change has been happening since creation, and it will continue into the future. Yes, we have made it worse with the recent footprints of modern ways, but that doesn't alter the fact that civilisations have always dealt with climate change. Aboriginal people in Australia have been through rising sea levels before, and stories about these events come from just about every nation. My Tagalaka countrymen told the story of Brolga Dreaming. The story came from the last ice age tens of thousands of years ago, when the sea level rose and flooded the neighbouring tribe's land. Tagalaka Country is higher than the coastal nations nearby, so the clan groups that lived by the sea came up and stayed on the high ground. This demonstrates resilience, with people helping each other and adapting to the power of nature's changes. There are so many stories about these events that teach us about adaptation, and yet people do not understand how important it is. Adaptation is the key to responding to both human-induced and natural climate change, but it is very hard for today's society to adapt if they do not know nature.

Ensuring healthy Country through Indigenous land management was an extremely important safeguard against unprecedented change. Moving camp in the wet season from the flood plains to higher ground was a sign of adaptation and the reason for the nomadic lifestyle. Looking after the animals and landscapes using traditional knowledge ensured that the natural environment did not become vulnerable to human negligence. Like the Old People taught me, always take notice of the land, otherwise you will get lost. That is what I have been doing through all my years of applying cultural burning, ever since the Elders gifted me with that ability.

After applying thousands of fires across many landscapes, I have not noticed any threat to the seasonal cultural burning windows. From droughts to periods of heavy rain, the changes in climate have not taken away the opportunity to apply the right fire that the land needs. There are so many opportunities to work on healing our natural world, but the chances slip by because people often don't see them. Knowing how to read Country provides solutions at a community level to help deal with climate crisis, if you know how to listen and act.

When Country is badly damaged, Mother Nature tries to step in. After the 2019–2020 mega fires in Australia, for example, massive rain events occurred to help heal the burns. It is not unusual for rain to come after a devastating fire. It's like the way we treat people when they are badly burned by dousing their burns in water. After those wildfires, from 2020 to 2024 much of the east coast of Australia experienced many seasons of heavy rain. My knowledge of applying traditional fire through the drought season was turned on its head. Usually, the window to burn during drier times starts in the wet season and ends before spring. However, the wetter period gave us the opportunity to burn right through the year, which I had not experienced before.

Western fire authorities informed the public that the land had been too wet to burn and they feared there would be major fires when it eventually dried out. They did not see that the wet weather was nature's healing process and the natural environment was benefiting greatly. The conditions actually gave us the opportunity to use fire in places that were too risky to burn when dry. During the wet season, the fire is sucked towards the ground, keeping it low and cool, even in the summer heat. It's as if nature has called, 'Time out!' to allow us to come in and start healing her wounds.

In the traditional times, the Old People would apply fire to storm-burn Country, which is an ecosystem that needs fire in the wet season. Today we use this season to treat all unhealthy ecosystems that have too much fuel or introduced weeds. This is an example of adaptation that aligns with healing Country. Traditional knowledge teaches us how to apply different timing to restore the identity of landscape as a healing solution. Then, once we see healthy Country come back, we return to the original practices and seasons our Ancestors applied. The healthy areas where the right native vegetation was growing did not burn because it was too green and healthy to carry fire at that time. This meant that the native animals and plants in these areas could go on with their usual cycles without being affected by the healing burns.

I have conducted burns during the wet season with many communities, and it is beautiful to watch the people walking through the landscape targeting the affected areas. There is almost no risk, as the natural firebreaks of green healthy landscapes and no-fire Country make it impossible for the fire to escape. In one case, we were able to burn multiple sites in one day without using any Western firefighting equipment. One person was able to walk safely through the land and burn many sites, knowing that the fires could not go beyond the sick vegetation.

While Mother Nature was replenishing the land with her magic rain season, we were giving her a helping hand to speed up the healing process and prepare the land for the effects of climate change. If I had my way, there would be thousands of practitioners walking through the land, treating these areas throughout the year, continuing stewardship and working in adaptation with Mother Nature to give her what she needs to deal with these unprecedented times. We may even give some places two or three patch burns over twelve months at different times of the year, to treat the diverse conditions of vegetation. To activate the land and assist the native vegetation and animals to restore themselves. To be in sync with nature's call for healing is what adaptation should be all about.

Today, in our disconnected world, people and government agencies are not taking the action needed during these healing periods. The Western system is so focused on its risk-driven methods of health and safety that it doesn't see what Mother Nature is offering. On a couple of occasions, we applied for a fire permit during those heavy wet seasons, and we were rejected by the fire warden. When we asked why, he said that it was too wet to burn. If the warden thought it was too wet to burn there should be no risk at all, and therefore no reason to reject the fire permit. It was another example of Western law getting in the way.

In general, people and governments are not fully aware of the many aspects of the climate change debate. In fact, the term 'climate change' has been spoiled to the point that we need to change the language, so that people can look at the problem through different perspectives. We need to restore biodiversity holistically and not argue only about a single component, such as carbon, based on satisfying accounting targets. If we restore the health of the land, then no doubt the carbon situation will naturally improve. It is also far better to focus on the indicators we can see in nature, rather than talk about carbon, which we can't see.

Like David Attenborough said in his 2020 documentary *A Life on Our Planet*, we must restore biodiversity before it is too late. It is as simple as that. Climate change can't be separated into different political issues. No one can deny the reality that our planet is facing decline. The bottom line is we have a lot of work to do in making way for positive change, and it can be the most exciting time if we all get on the same page. It really boils down to whether or not humans are prepared to sacrifice some of their privileges to give back to nature. To save what we have left and restore biodiversity on this planet we call home. This is the test that we cannot fail.

CHAPTER 18

To the bone

Back in 2006, I was privileged to go with an Elder from Cape York in northern Australia, to visit the old settlements way out bush where he had grown up. We had to go by helicopter as there was no other way to get to that area, which is surrounded by crocodile-infested wetlands. When we landed, the Old Man walked over to what was once his childhood home. He slowly folded his tall bony frame down into the long, overgrown grass and sat cross-legged in the shade. 'This is where I grew up, boy, long time ago now.' Going by the Old Man's age, I guessed that the small settlement was active in the 1940s.

He pointed his long fingers to some stumps in the ground. 'Over there was my house and over that way was where my uncle lived. We used to live off the land, get rations sent in by the white fellas and carry our water from the well,' he said in a gravelly voice. I sat next to him looking at the old stumps, trying to imagine the tin shack that once stood there. Glancing around, I noticed something on the ground so I walked over to take a closer look.

'What is this?' I asked.

'That's a typewriter,' the Old Man replied.

I went on to ask him what an old typewriter was doing way out here, and the Elder said it had belonged to his sister. He pointed to a mound of dirt not far from where I was standing. 'That's her grave over there. She died a long time ago.'

I gave a moment of silence in respect and then asked him what she did with the typewriter.

'She used to run the post office, type all the letters and send them everywhere,' he said proudly.

'A post office!'

'Yeah, boy, when we were here not many white fellas lived with us. We ran the place ourselves.'

The Old Man showed me where they'd had the veggie garden, and he then took me to see where the rest of the houses had stood in the little Aboriginal settlement. It must have been amazing to live there, as the tidal rivers close by were filled with an abundance of fish and a lot of crocodiles.

'Why did you have to leave this place?' I asked.

The Elder said that the police came and told them they had to go to the new settlement built for Aboriginal people. Once his family were given the orders to march, they left and never returned. He told me that they didn't manage their own community anymore after that. It was operated by non-Indigenous caretakers who employed Indigenous staff.

After that day, I asked many Elders from various places around Australia about those early settlement times. I learned that the white settlers had their own towns with laws to restrict Aboriginal people from living there too. Many Elders told me stories of those hard-working days. They had a lot of bone, which meant they were tough and resilient. Many of the Old People before and during the early settlement times were physically active and knowledgeable. They had seen the worst happen to their people and Country, but always referred to those days as the good days.

That says a lot about the times we are experiencing today and why the old ways hold important values for our future. During the colonial times in Australia, many clan groups from different regions were placed together in one settlement away from their homelands. I have visited many of those old camps from the early days, and at most of them I saw evidence of gardens and infrastructure. My grandmother was a gardener in her homelands up north, and she also had goats and chickens to feed the families.

I have heard stories of a few Aboriginal people in areas further south who ran their own farms. But once they showed that they could adapt to Western ways and farm productively, the government took their farms from them. Most of my grandmother's generation worked for very low wages and did not get full pay rights until 1968. When the Western law for equal pay came into effect, most Aboriginal people lost their low-paid jobs and were forced onto welfare. My nanna had to leave her Tagalaka homelands along with other families because there was suddenly no work to support them. This happened in many remote towns, and the people were forced onto settlements and into towns. The Aboriginal people couldn't access their traditional land in some places because it was locked up by private and corporate landholders. Most remote Aboriginal communities became dependent on welfare, and many had non-Indigenous caretakers running their community amenities. The Elders' traditional knowledge and skills began to slip away, one generation at a time.

The Old People from those hard-working days have watched as the times and conditions changed to what they are today. It went from people living with no money, having to work hard for rations and gardening for food, to the generations that got paid for doing very little at all. The garden foods and traditional hunting diets changed to fast foods and addictive products. That created a downward spiral of health complications and chaotic ways of life, which disempowered Aboriginal people within mainstream society. The Old People used to say all the time, 'Where are all the good working men and women gone?'

At one stage in the 1990s, we had a good 'Work-for-the-Dole' program, which was a community development employment program initiated by the Australian Government. It was through this program that I got my first job as a community ranger. That program was working well in the region I lived in, but then the government closed it down. Instead, they paid people the same amount without those people working at all. Many Elders I knew didn't like their community living on welfare, and they were even more worried for those people who suffered from addictions. The challenges of trying to pull people out of a life of disadvantage were too big for many Elders to overcome. When you combine that with Western laws limiting the way Indigenous people could live, it became incredibly hard to live a healthy, independent life. Drugs, alcohol, junk food, and the influence of social media trap a lot of people in a state of vulnerability. At the same time, a proportion of non-Indigenous Australians judge Aboriginal people and claim that they are lazy and dysfunctional.

To be seen by society as a burden or unequal can only make it harder to rise from rock bottom. No matter how much money the government throws at the welfare problem today, that strategy will only make it grow bigger. Instead, the approach to welfare should be based on supporting the aspirations of the community and creating jobs to heal Country, culture and community. Allowing people to receive money without doing any service for the community or Country does not help to solve the problems at hand. This social dilemma also affects many non-Indigenous people who have lost a lot of the historical knowledge and skills of their forebears. In fact, this trend is affecting more and more people every day around the globe.

The current governing systems have certainly weakened much of our general society. Many countries have become so risk-averse that basic work practices and skills are highly regulated, making simple tasks complicated. Of course, it is essential to work safely, but some rules and regulations can prevent us from reaching our potential. Often those laws override commonsense and contribute to making humanity and our planet even more vulnerable. In one example, I was working with a community seeking to do a cool burn on Country that was very weedy, and we needed good wind gusts to push the fire along. But the fire warden said the wind exceeded their limit and would not issue a permit for the burn, resulting in us missing our burning window. There was no risk at all because the land was wet and green, which made it non-flammable and perfect for the burn. Over the years I have watched restrictions and bureaucracy grow, and the opportunities to do the work that's necessary fall away. That results in wasted time and money, as well as problems left to linger so the conditions only become worse.

In many cases, programs to manage the land that could prevent catastrophes have been stalled by government agencies as they nitpick over the possibility of liabilities. That leaves people doing nothing and simply waiting for the next disaster. The way our society limits our abilities has already led to losing old knowledge and practices, and will make it harder to build a proactive culture going into the future.

Moreover, it costs money to comply with so many health and safety laws. And complying with regulations from more than one government or corporate agency is particularly complicated. Insurance companies' requirements and high fees can also make it impossible for trained practitioners to do simple cultural burns to protect Country. Sometimes insurance companies won't cover activities like cultural burning at all. Then a big wildfire comes and destroys thousands of houses, leading to massive losses. How can we look after Country and limit the threats if we can't get insurance to prevent disasters? Government and insurance requirements can lead to endless paper trails that make it a nightmare to do one task. The bubble-wrap situation we find ourselves in will only get worse.

With Indigenous fire management, we must burn the land when Country tells us to. Skilled practitioners should be able to apply fire whenever landscapes show the signs of being ready. Instead, Western policies get in the way and nature's calling is missed.

If we are going to be successful in healing the planet, we need to ease out of the risk-averse culture and bring in some logic and common sense. Training cultural fire practitioners is just one example of how proactive management can reduce risks and increase efficiency. The safest thing you can have is not legislation and safety equipment, it is knowledge of the land. When you work with knowledge of the land, the Country is the boss; if you work from the book of legislation, then the system is the boss.

Over the years, I have found good practice in crafting restoration programs led by Indigenous knowledge. When Indigenous peoples can effectively revive their cultural practices, then the solutions can be shared with the broader community. We can build an inclusive strategy from the ground up by respecting people and place.

Mentoring Indigenous individuals and communities to help them learn and embrace their cultural practices is important work and I find it very rewarding. I have seen individual practitioners excel in their skills and grow culturally, spiritually, mentally and physically by learning from Country. Once people see the land through the lens of traditional knowledge, they tend to change in a natural way. The adopted habit of fear begins to fall away and they have a profound sense of purpose and responsibility. It brings a sense of belonging that enables the Ancestors and the land to work through them.

Knowledge is beautifully powerful when it is applied through the natural world in the way of connecting with our Ancestors and rediscovering our identities. I have met some people who were terrified of snakes and would never walk through the bush. Within the first hour of learning about Country, they were striding through scrubland confidently and with interest. Having a stronger understanding of the land made them feel safer and more connected to their surroundings.

For many young people, a job that requires cutting out thousands of hectares of weedy, invasive vegetation could seem just too hard. But when the practitioners become a part of the land, they can't wait to start doing the work. It becomes their dream job, and they are learning their traditional knowledge. While mentoring and working alongside these crews, I began to see that the young people were motivated to put some bone into their work. It was empowering to see good, hard-working men and women, just like the Old People wanted. That is the type of work ethic we need for our future generations – when we are working together for a greater purpose rather than just the pay packet alone.

In some ways it can become a problem when people work solely to make money and have no interest in working to benefit others and the planet. These are not the workers Mother Nature is looking for, nor does this attitude help to build successful community-driven outcomes. Of course, workers need to be paid and their rights protected, but sometimes Western laws can limit productivity.

The Western law of having a board to lead community-based organisations, for example, can lead to benefits or problems. It helps to have a good board of directors who have a clear vision and bring everyone together. But I have heard stories about directors who think they are more important than the rest of the community and insist on getting more privileges. Bad directors can mislead an organisation, direct funds so the money lands in their own pockets or make claims that are untrue. A good board of directors will put their shoulders 100 per cent behind the workers and the community and share their passions, visions and goals.

Yes, we need money to survive, and that is why we need thousands of jobs to support hard-working individuals and families. But to get there we should be prepared to put in more than we receive, if we are able to, and make sacrifices that will bring the rewards into the future. In the early years of trying to get the traditional burns program going, I worked for very little pay and sometimes for nothing at all. I was sure that money would come eventually, even if it was just enough for my family and me to get by and live a happy life. The spirit of the Old People has shown me that you get back as much as you put in and that in the end, the universe will provide.

When we work for Country and spirit, we find ourselves in the place we want to be. Teaching this to the younger generations is vital, as it shows them where to find the ultimate security for life. To reconnect with the land, to sing songs while we chip away the intergenerational targets and, above all, to have the bone to stand up and endure the challenges along the way. If we can achieve this outlook in the new jobs of the future, then we will be on our way to healing our world – making it healthy and prosperous for all.

CHAPTER 19

The planet is us

You may have worked out by now that the Indigenous way of thinking is often opposite to the way many societies see the world today. And the way modern humanity thinks can often be the complete opposite to the physics of natural lore. Most things are back to front, upside down or the wrong way around, and that is the weirdest phenomenon of our modern times. In most cases, the solution to a problem can be found by simply turning the situation the other way round. So you do something in the opposite way to how it is currently done, which may have caused the disorder in the first place. Proactive versus reactive. Connected versus disconnected.

The problem is when something that is upside down is enforced by law, and then it is eventually accepted in modern thinking as the norm. When that happens, we end up with a divided society, and when the disconnected side becomes dominant, the natural world will be negatively affected. For example, the Indigenous way of thinking about fire is that it is a part of nature, while modern society has a fear of fire and regards it as a threat. As a result, we see more destruction from wildfires.

The Elders were so knowledgeable and knew so much about the land, sky and seas. Now many people look at the bush, for example, and only see sticks, grass and trees. The rapid loss of both knowledge and human connection with the world is alarming. We now live in a society where artificial intelligence (AI) is far greater than natural intelligence. What has been introduced to us as a convenience has the potential to become a vicious cancer. AI is like an impersonation of humanity, and it is slowly entrenching itself in our lives. AI and other major changes to our society can lead to fear and uncertainty. That's why it is so important to recognise that the natural world holds the truth of where we went wrong and how we can get back on track. The answers are right in front of us.

One time, I was in Finland and my Indigenous friend there took me to see a rock-art site. The first thing that struck me was how similar it was to our cultural sites in Australia. The only difference was the type of animals, plants and spirits depicted on the wall. Rock art can be found on every continent except for Antarctica. Then again, who knows what lies under all that ice, which has captured our footprints in time. The rock-art sites are an ancient reference to remind us that people have evolved on this planet. It shows us that across the world, we once lived with the land, and now humanity is slowly being disconnected from the roots of nature.

I have heard many stories from traditional cultures about how Indigenous people were stripped of their land and traditions by the Church. Churches were built on sacred Indigenous grounds to replace spiritually with religion – like the old saying: 'Religion was given to the First Peoples of the world in exchange for the land.' The sacredness of nature was considered evil and devalued in ways that disrupted thousands of years of human occupation. Indigenous people were ordered not to worship the natural world, but to accept religion and to kneel before the Church. It was not a request; it was an order from the high priests and others, including the government. They drew the people into the churches so they could no longer see the land and filled them with fear if they did not follow.

We are told that heaven is a beautiful place we go to when we die. That idea overlooks the heaven on Earth that is around us already. It is a miracle and one of the greatest of wonders to be living on such a beautiful planet. Creating a society that is disconnected from nature makes it easier for the system to suck the Earth dry of its riches. Many religions support taking care of nature, but not many teach us how to do that as a spiritual, cultural practice.

The whole world is ultimately dealing with the changes brought by colonisation. The mindset of the colonisers was that they were superior to the ancient cultures of the world. This misconception still feeds the beast that continues to suck the life from our planet, yet the reality is that those who think they are superior will eventually end up in the same place as the oppressed.

The antidote is to restore humanity's respect for natural intelligence. That can be achieved by working with Mother Nature, so she can thrive, and by understanding that we are all indigenous to this planet. Evolution is the foundation of our existence, and every race of people contributes important values to the future of humanity. The Western and Eastern cultures bring their technical innovations to the world and have contributed greatly to human advancement. Our challenge is to ensure that technology serves us while we stay in control of our destinies. We must be careful not to lose our core human values and our natural world along the way. That is where Indigenous knowledge can help with connecting people to the planet, through reviving practices and ways of thinking. We should use the philosophies of natural and cultural lore to guide us as we use technology and artificial intelligence.

Many technical advancements are used in ways that do not consider the lores of nature and the health of our environment. The car spews fossil fuels from its exhaust while killing a large tally of native animals by hitting them along the highways. Household and industrial waste, including microplastics, pollutes the world. Poisons sprayed across crops to control pests also harm humans and animals. Earth-moving and extraction machinery create runoff, turning clean rivers muddy and brown. The list of offences to Mother Nature rolls out the courtroom door and onto the street.

Going out into space is done by burning tonnes of fossil fuels, and space junk is left orbiting our planet. Even the night sky is polluted with internet satellite constellations. The irony of it all is that humans got all these expensive toys from Mother Nature in the first place, yet she is not a beneficiary. Humans today don't understand the right way to live with each other and nature. Now we have AI coming along and it could bring even more problems, if we are not careful.

The knowledge of nature is where the greatest innovations can come from if we take the time to understand it better. If humans can create technology that does not harm the planet, this would take us to the next level of intelligence. Ancient knowledges from around the world can guide us to greater heights now and into the future. We can shoot for the stars, but we must never forget where we come from. Imagine if technologically advanced societies listened to the wisdom of the Ancestors' knowledge systems. We are in a race against time to heal our planet, with a young knowledge system in charge that has greatly contributed to the decline.

There are many people seeking traditional knowledge for answers to the environmental and social challenges we face. We've gone full circle, where we look back to the old knowledge that was almost erased by the present. The test for humanity is to turn things up the right way, to put nature first to restore the health of the people. When we look at the land, we should be able to see ourselves, almost as if we are gazing at our reflection in the water.

Trees are the lungs of the earth, contributing to the clean fresh breath of life. We are like the trees in many ways. The bronchiole branches in our lungs look just like trees and they too play the role of enabling oxygen to support life. Sometimes our lungs can get damaged by inhaling poisonous smoke or chemicals. Similarly, we can damage nature's atmosphere when we carelessly spray poisons, pollute the air and water, or allow wildfires to burn our landscape to a cinder.

If we don't look after ourselves, we can become susceptible to illnesses. Then we will need a treatment regime to heal. The same applies to Mother Earth when she is suffering from the weeds, the land clearing, the pollution, the wildfires and other disturbances that cause her symptoms. So many modern diseases are caused by the poisons that we consume through our skin, lungs and mouths. We know that we will live a short life if our bodies fill up with poisons in this way, and the same applies to Mother Nature. We are not opposite to nature.

Ancient cultures have strong spiritual relationships with nature and treat the Earth with respect. If you measure that against the way modern humanity is treating the world, we seem more like spoiled brats taking the gift of life for granted. We think we know everything but end up getting into trouble all the time. Even when we clearly know we are doing the wrong thing, we still do it anyway. Just as young children don't always listen to the advice of their parents, young knowledge systems do not listen the voices of ancient wisdom.

We have ended up in a situation where we are like the good and bad bacteria that live in our bodies. The bad bacteria are the greedy people contributing to destroying our Mother Earth, and the good bacteria are those people who act to heal and protect her. The good bacteria try to fight off the bad to restore balance within the body. This does not only apply to healing our environment but also our society, as the good bacteria tries to overcome the bad until it is completely washed out of the system. Restoring the balance starts with educating each other until we are no longer good and bad bacteria, but red and white blood cells instead: two separate cells of different colours that work together to keep the body alive and well. Black and white, left and right, man and woman – just like those red and white blood cells, opposites can work together to keep Mother Earth alive.

It is nice to know that the Earth is a living being, just like you and me. But there is one thing we should all remember: there are billions of us – just like the billions of cells that run around inside each of us – but only one of her. We expect our cells to do their job well, so we can live a long, healthy life. It is our responsibility to do the same for Mother Nature, by keeping the balance right. For most people it is hard to think about where to start, with so many complicated challenges on our hands. There is so much work to do on a planet that is so big.

The process of healing can only start one job at a time, day by day, no matter how big or small. If we wake up each day with the goal to care for the Earth and do what we can, then she will improve her immune system and start to heal. When we look at the work required to achieve this goal into the future, it all starts with giving our planet love. That is what people need to give each other and themselves too. Things won't improve if we continue to live opposite to the natural world by fearing fire, declaring war with nature, fighting each other, or thinking that climate change is unavoidable doom and gloom. If you treat any living thing like the enemy, it will become your enemy and that is the opposite to peace.

To restore hope, we simply need to get on with the job of cleaning up the mess, no matter who is responsible. You have a choice: be the one cleaning up, or the one being cleaned up. The transition is inevitable and needs to be put into action before things get worse and the condition of our world becomes terminal. Every person alive today, no matter what age, needs to be the turning point for humanity to see the world the right way up again – to listen to our Mother and the oldest of her children, to learn the knowledge and work together with open minds. To activate communities to look after their homelands and each other in ways that empower the change needed for generations to come.

In this universe, anything is possible if we listen to what has been learned from the oldest of cultures to the new. We cannot go wrong if we learn to be one with nature. We can overcome the fires, improve our waters, stop war and erase famine if we turn everything that is opposite the right way around. The only way to make this possible is to know that the planet is us; it is the heaven in which we are already living. So let's turn everything that is upside down the right way up again and know that we are the planet and the planet is us, as one and for all.

CHAPTER 20

The knowledge that underpins us all

Early on, when I had just started to run Indigenous fire workshops around Australia, I was invited to do a particular cultural burning presentation. The venue was the local hall and there were over 100 people in the audience, including various stakeholders from the community. I went up onto the stage and after the host introduced me, I talked about the concept of Aboriginal fire management.

I spoke with a strong passion, as usual, and the presentation seemed to go well. When it was over, the audience applauded while I walked down the stairs at the front of the stage. As I headed towards the front door, a woman sitting in the crowd got my attention. She was looking at me as if we were long-lost friends. I nodded to her and was going to keep walking, but she reached out and gently grabbed my arm to guide me into her space.

'I have something to tell you,' she said, in the sweetest voice.

Her smile was friendly and she seemed to be a warm, loving lady. She was middle-aged and mixed-race. Her Caucasian husband sitting next to her also gave me a warm smile but left it to his wife to speak.

'I have to tell you something that might be a bit hard to believe,' she said. 'When you were up on the stage doing your talk, there was a spirit standing behind you the whole time.' She paused briefly.

'It was an old woman,' the lady went on to say, in a reassuring way.

My mind went straight to my Aboriginal grandmother, because I had been brought up connecting with Aboriginal spirituality. But then the lady told me that the spirit was an Ancestor from my father's side. That was a surprise as I hadn't learned a lot from my father about his Ancestors. He couldn't tell me much about the cultural side of his bloodlines except that his grandparents came from Norway or Sweden. The Steffensen name is Scandinavian. I had visited that region while working with the Sámi people in northern Finland and a friend took me to see the Arctic shores.

The lady said that the spirit woman was wearing what looked like old-fashioned European clothes.

'She wants me to tell you two things that you need to know. Firstly, she wants you to lighten up,' the lady said with a little smile.

I accepted that advice with an open heart; I was a little too passionate and persistent during my younger days. The lady looked at me and drew me closer to deliver her last message.

'The second thing she wants you to know is that there is a deeper knowledge, far greater than what you already know.'

She let my arm go and settled back into her seat, giving the warmest of smiles. 'That's all she wanted me to tell you. I hope that makes sense for you,' she said.

I thanked the lady for the message and said goodbye to her and her husband. Then I walked outside to a park bench on the front lawn to sit down in the fresh air to process what had just happened. It was one of those special moments in life, and I was surprised to be given a riddle by an Ancestor from my father's side.

Knowledge deeper than what I was already learning and practising, derived from the oldest culture in the world. The riddle stayed in my mind for a few years, along with an image of an old European Ancestor who had stood with me that day. It made my hair stand on end just thinking about it, and the advice drew me to explore who I was within my own spirit. It gave me a sense of excitement, connectedness and a divine feeling of peacefulness, all at the same time. I knew the answer would eventually come to light. There is always more work to do, and I would have to be patient and gain the experience I needed to find the answer that I was destined to learn.

I thought about all I had learned from my mentor and the Indigenous communities I've visited in Australia and overseas, and the stories they've shared with me from their Ancestors. As I have discovered, there are so many similarities between landscapes and cultures from one side of the world to the other. I thought about the many countries that experience similar challenges, both socially and environmentally. The need for global mentorship to move away from a world suffering a state of decline also came to mind. Then I thought about the beautiful people I had met from all walks of life who share the same love and aspirations for Country and culture. The fact that there are so many good people in the world is another indication that we share a connected existence.

One time I received an invitation to do an audio interview with the BBC News network in Scotland. It was a live interview with a panel of Scottish scientists; they were in the room together and I was streaming in on my phone. The host asked me some questions about traditional land management practices, including cultural fire. In my response, I spoke about my experiences from Aboriginal Australia and how the land was managed culturally before colonisation. Then I explained the challenges along with the good work that was happening through reviving traditional fire practices.

When my interview ended, the host thanked me for my input and I went to leave the call. She then turned to the panel of scientists and asked them, 'What do you think of what Victor said?'

One of the scientists answered, 'We used to look after the land with cultural practices before we were assimilated under a foreign empire. We had cultural connections to the land and traditional practices to care for our Country.'

The panel members did not say much about fire but talked about their land and culture with great passion. That was all I heard before my phone line was disconnected.

It was refreshing and empowering to hear those few words outside of my own Country and culture. Words that revealed the ancient cultural connection the scientists had with their ancestral homeland. It is evident that most cultures around the world had a greater connection with our Mother Earth prior to colonisation.

I also did a podcast with people from England who were interested in traditional knowledge for the wellbeing of their natural landscapes. And I was featured in a magazine from London called *Where the Leaves Fall*, which had a focus on culturally restoring the planet. It was good to see the interest coming from one of the biggest colonising countries in the world. Recently I have received requests from communities in Japan and Italy that want to have their Indigenous fire practices revived. Talking to people at the community level this way is exactly how these conversations should start. I learned from people in Italy how they traditionally used particular native plants for craft practices, but now those plants are becoming scarce. I've heard similar stories, sharing knowledge and concerns, from many Indigenous people worldwide. Listening to people from different nations talking about the connection they have with their Country takes me to the same place – it is the answer to the riddle.

The deep wisdom – which is greater than anyone – is the knowledge that underpins us all. The connection that all humans have with Mother Nature stretches across the origins of humanity. To restore the old knowledge systems and connections on a global scale may help humanity find its way home. Reviving cultural fire in Canada with the support of traditional knowledge from Aboriginal Australia, for example, was powerfully awakening. A deeper knowledge not only reveals cultural similarities with nature but also exposes our collective responsibility of caring for the planet. We need to unlock the blueprints of humanity through Mother Nature and see ourselves in each other. It will be amazing to revive the original practices globally and build a network of international enlightenment. What has been achieved through our work in Canada shows that it can be done with many traditional cultures across the world. Taking a global approach of reconnecting to our roots will help us through the struggles that countries face on their own. Addressing the problems collectively can initiate a crucial healing process. In the work we've already done, we can see the benefits we can achieve, and if we can make it work with fire, then it can work with every other field of philosophy and practice.

The revival of traditional knowledge solutions across cultures will be good for many Westernised countries. It will help people to understand that we are all reconnecting. That we come from the roots of our own unique motherlands and share a deep history that is culturally closer to nature. In multicultural countries, people who are not Indigenous to that place can finally learn about their own bloodlines and backgrounds. This may help them to learn and understand the Indigenous culture of the land that they're now living on.

It would be revolutionary for Australians whose Ancestors were from another country to find out how people from their ancestral homelands are reviving their cultural practices. Maybe the growing awareness of our ancestral roots will encourage people to learn more about who we really are. That may lead to a greater respect for the Indigenous peoples of the lands that others are so privileged to benefit from. If humanity has lost its way, then it makes sense to go back to the beginning, to retrace our steps and pick ourselves up again. It will certainly increase our chances of living on the planet for thousands of years more, and longer if possible.

Education is crucial; it has always been the way knowledge has been passed down for generations. I love to write children's books to share the knowledge and help pave the way for the next generations. I listened to the spirits when they asked me to lighten up a bit. That is exactly why it is so important to put children first – because teaching the young people is a lot more fun than trying to make change through the system. It needs to be fun if we are going to take on what can feel like a daunting task; otherwise we are all just hitting our heads against a brick wall. If you are having a laugh each day about life, then you are certainly doing something the right way.

When it comes to understanding traditional knowledge, adults are at the same stage of learning as our children are. So we might as well build a positive healing future with children being far more involved than what they are at present. Involving the children is one of the most important aspirations for Indigenous Elders around the world. They want children to grow into adults who can carry on the traditions that form our long-term goals and responsibilities. To uphold a continuous culture of living harmoniously with nature, instead of falling into the condition of a disorientated species. It is our Elders who we respect the most, but it is our children who must succeed beyond the stars.

We need to teach children about their responsibility of healing Country, with modern minds nurtured by ancient wisdom. This starts by simply ensuring that our children are outside more than inside the house, trapped by digital screens.

My mother used to kick me out of the house when I was kid to go and play down by the river. She did not want us sitting around watching television or playing video games. I think that following her example might be a good idea in any day and age.

The main aim for creating the organisation Living Knowledge Network is to help young people find amazing opportunities to be the solution. To create the dream jobs that people will cherish and that will empower them within this modern world. To offer them jobs they never dreamed they would have or would be able to do. To give young people perspectives on life that are wider and higher than any mountain. For them all to become anything they want to be and to thrive in the name of Mother Nature and the spirits.

We can teach children how everything is connected and how to think in circles rather than in a linear way. This is how Mother Nature taught Indigenous Elders to become walking encyclopaedias. That is why you may have read about key points of traditional knowledge repeated a few times throughout this book on different subjects. That repetition is intentional. This is because everything is connected – you may hear it many times, but you will learn a little more about it each time.

In the Knowledge Map, which appears on pages 258–9, everything is connected through a vast kinship of co-benefits. The circular design of the map is how information should sit in our heads when thinking about any subject. This interrelated way of thinking comes from nature, therefore it is a formula that will keep going and going. Like my mentor said to me so many years ago, 'When I die, the land will keep on teaching you.'

Once you learn the language of Country, it will talk to you for the rest of your life. That is the security that future generations need, and it is nature's gift that every child should receive. That is to build a strong cultural connection to the land with natural intelligence infused within our reality and purpose. If we can pass this onto the next generations, then they will be able to improve it into the future.

I am passing onto the next generations the knowledge the Old People taught me. Like keeping sourdough culture alive for baking bread, keeping traditional knowledge alive will enable the next generations to rise. If the sourdough culture is lost, then the bread that uses a process thousands of years old cannot be baked anymore. Children are integral to the ongoing culture, to help the knowledge of humanity grow again.

The older generations also have an important part to play; we can make positive change happen now rather than letting the system dominate. All we need to do is let go of control and ego to allow opportunity to flourish. It is really that simple, but the hardest part is to break out of the social mindsets we are currently trapped in – the mindsets that obscure the bigger picture and have deprived us of so much opportunity for too long.

For private landholders to help by making their property available for fire workshops to inform people in their region. For farmers to trial ways to improve agriculture with traditional local knowledge. To have industries helping the natural environment thrive by involving community stewardship. For teachers to show children the various solutions to heal the land and connect them with the aspirations of their communities. By growing your own food that is aligned with the land and sharing

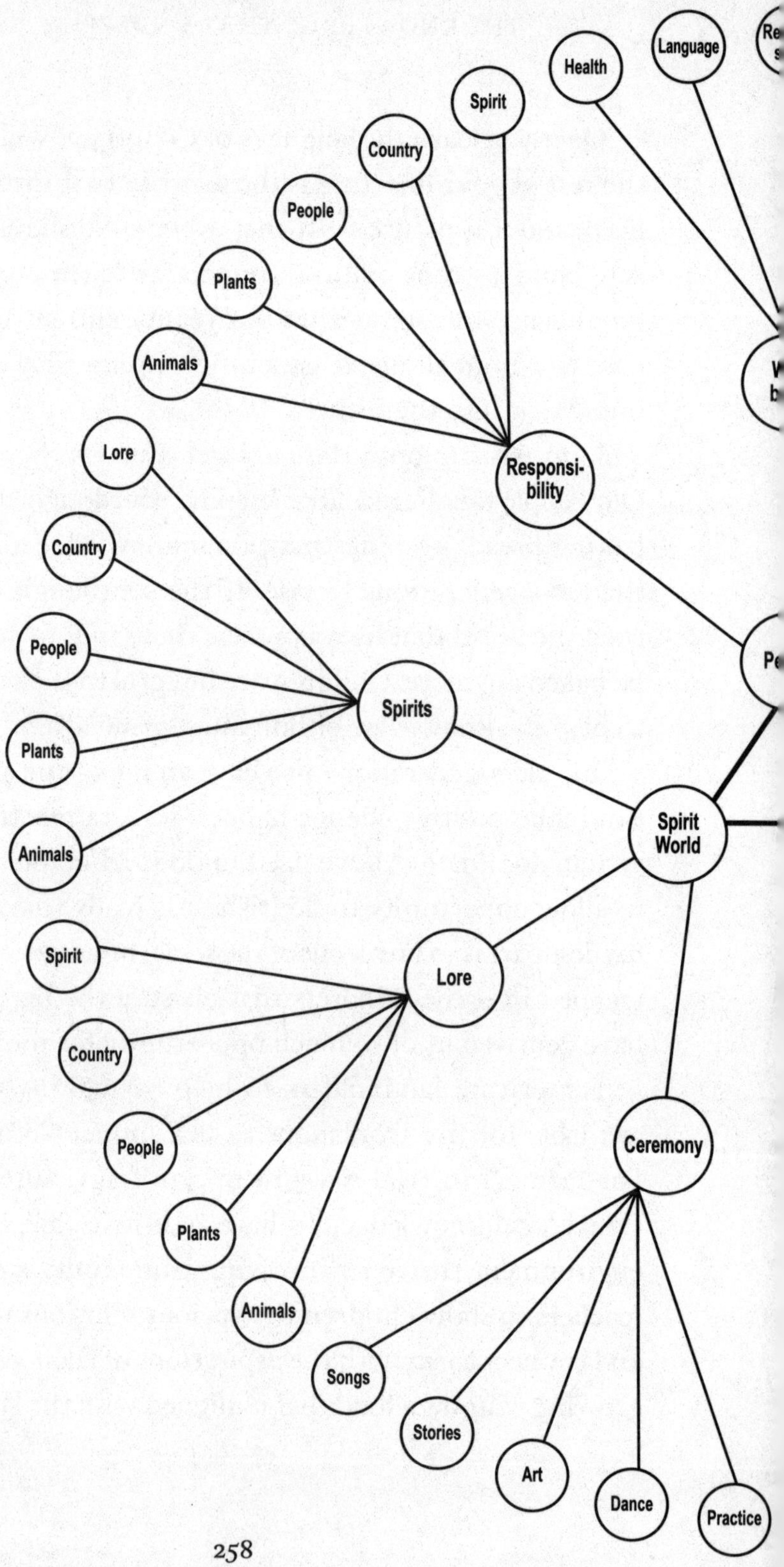
Health
Language
Spirit
Country
People
Plants
Animals
Responsi-
bility
Lore
Country
People
Plants
Animals
Spirits
Spirit
World
Spirit
Country
People
Plants
Animals
Lore
Ceremony
Songs
Stories
Art
Dance
Practice

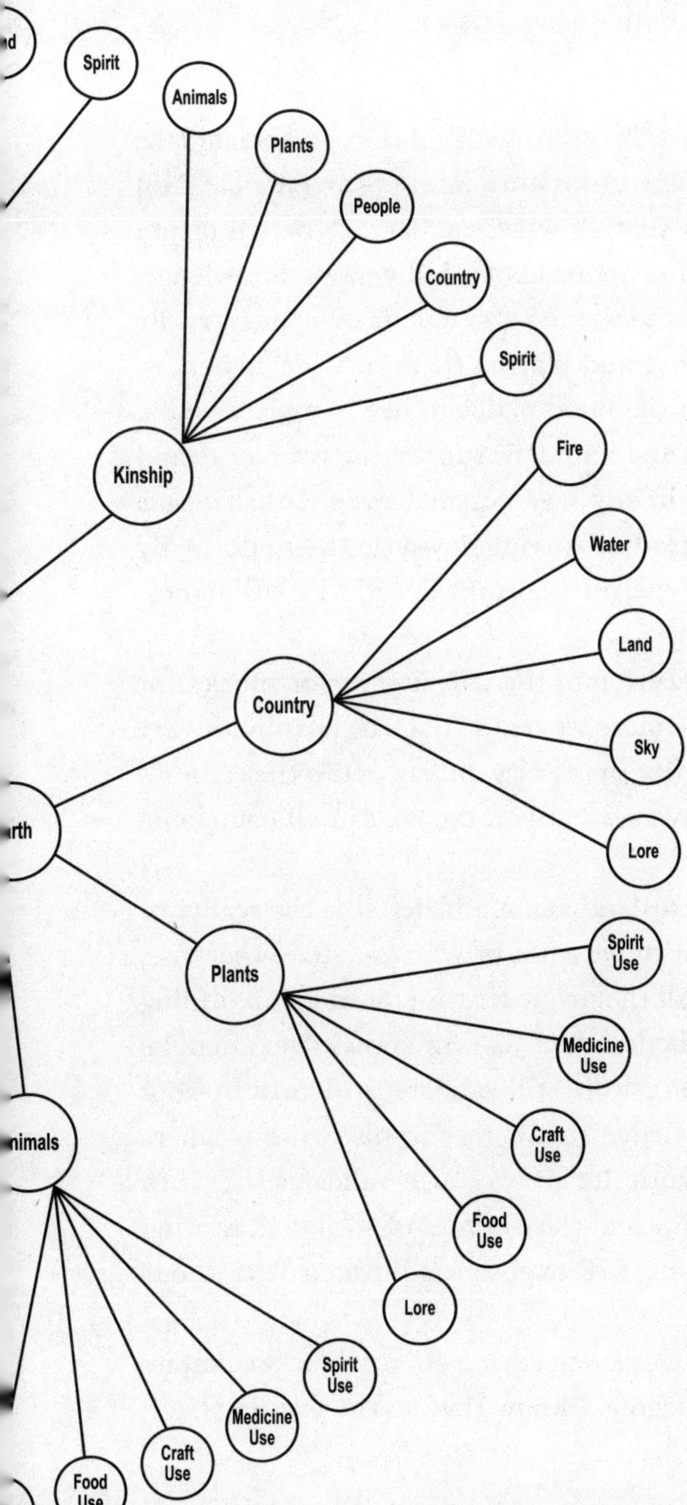

The Knowledge Map

it with your neighbours. By visiting an old tree, an ancient lake or just keeping connected to nature in any way possible. Not being wasteful, but by sharing what you have, if there is plenty to go around. Learning more about Indigenous knowledge, which hopefully leads to learning about your own ancestry. By writing songs about love and playing them to wide audiences. By moving away from the flood plains to live in a place where you are tucked up safe and sound. By supporting your local land restoration programs in any way possible, even if that means talking people up instead of looking down on their efforts. By bringing in love and generosity sprinkled with the willingness to learn open-mindedly.

The further we venture into the amazing opportunities for us all to contribute, the more we realise that the possibilities are endless. Whether you live in the city or way out in the country, no matter who you are or what you do, we can all contribute and belong.

The knowledge of the land is not a belief; it is the reality of our natural world and the essence of who we are. Otherwise, it would not produce all the magic that is embedded in healing people and Country. Thousands of years of knowledge cannot be wrong, especially when nature still validates its worth in front of our eyes. The knowledge that comes from nature is where we will always find truth. Its absence also validates the truth with our planet's decline and the disorder of society. Restoring the knowledge of nature will expose the illusions within our modern world.

I sit here finishing this story with a good vibration, despite the challenges we are facing. I know that it is an exciting time, a time of awakening to discover our fullest potential. I am excited about the great work all of us can do now. To find the commonalities between our vast variety of cultures and with each other. To reclaim what we have been deprived of and to put back what people and place need to thrive in harmony.

It is time for people to turn the projections of fear into the fun process of healing and creating prosperity for all. A time for us to be proactive and nourish ourselves to the point of never looking back. I know it is possible because the transformation has already begun. There are so many good people around the world ready to connect and work together. All that is required is to open our minds, be rid of fear and simply let the healing opportunities flow endlessly, to flood the world with the positivity of love.

To realign humanity with nature is to revive the knowledge that underpins us all.

ACKNOWLEDGEMENTS

I would like to thank everyone who has been a part of this honourable journey in some way, shape or form. There are too many good people and communities to thank. They all know who they are and how much they are appreciated. To all my friends, brothers and sisters who have shared this journey with me and who continue to strive alongside me, I am truly humbled and blessed. I would like to acknowledge my mentors, the late Dr George Musgrave (Snr) and the late Dr Tommy George (Snr), for believing in me and in the journey we started together and vowed to complete. You are forever in my heart, and I will always be proud of what we accomplished in those earlier years. In great gratitude to my own family who have always been there for me, including my extended families. I would like to acknowledge our Aboriginal family connections of the Tagalaka people and pay my full respects to all countrymen and women associated. This book is written in the hope that we can restore our cultural knowledge and create opportunities for Tagalaka people to return to Country with prospects for the future.

A special thanks to the Firesticks organisation (Living Knowledge Place) and all the staff and communities involved in Australia and internationally. We have all kicked amazing goals in restoring our beautiful people, culture and Country. It is through our work together that we shine and continue to inspire the world with what we do with love for community and Country. This book is written to empower the work you do and to acknowledge that you are all valued and on the right path to autonomy and cultural restoration. Thanks to Craig North and the entire leadership team for making the organisation what it is today – an organisation with integrity that honours the knowledge, our Elders and what we stand for.

I would like to acknowledge the Yunesit'in and Xeni communities of the Tsilhqot'in Nations in British Columbia, Canada, and the journey we continue to restore the cultural fire on your traditional homelands. Special thanks to Russell Myers Ross for leading the charge for his people and keeping the cultural fire alive as one of the leading traditional fire projects in Canada that is fully Indigenous led. A special thanks also to William Nikolakis (Billy) and the Gathering Voices Society team for making the fire program in Canada possible. Without you, amazing opportunities to demonstrate this special transfer of traditional knowledge from one side of the world to the other would not be possible.

I would like to acknowledge the farmers, organisations and corporations that work with Firesticks and continue to be involved in changing the narrative about what it means to respect Country and community. A special shout-out to all the private landholders who have supported the local Indigenous communities in their regions to instigate innovative programs to restore their areas. Without you, many of the great initiatives we have accomplished for both Indigenous and non-Indigenous people would not be possible.

Special thanks to Melissa Kayser and the team at Murdoch Books for making this book possible and getting this story out into the world. Thanks to Laura Thomas and Sarah Odgers for the book's cover design. Thanks also to Bernadette Foley for being the editor of this important piece of work.

I would also like to thank the readers who will take action to get the good work going after reading this book. It is the people who need to take charge to achieve positive change.

Finally, I would like to thank Mother Earth and the spirits for teaching me throughout my life and giving me the purpose to do this work within this lifetime. There is nothing greater than being with creation itself and I am truly thankful and blessed to be working for the most important employer of all. Thank you for showing us that we exist as one in this beautiful world, universe and beyond. I look forward to continuing this amazing journey with you and onwards to eternity.

INDEX

Note: Page numbers in *italics* refer to illustrations.

Victor Steffensen is an author, filmmaker, musician and traditional knowledge practitioner. He is a descendant of the Tagalaka people from North Queensland and respectfully acknowledges the European bloodlines within his family tree.

Much of Victor's work is based on the arts and reviving practical traditional knowledge values, particularly Aboriginal fire and land management, with Aboriginal and non-Indigenous communities. He is the co-founder of the Firesticks Alliance (Living Knowledge Place), which involves a large community network across Australia and internationally. Victor was gifted an Honorary Doctorate of Science from James Cook University for his work. He is the author of *Fire Country* and the children's books *Looking After Country with Fire, The Trees* and *Animals on Country*. Through his artistic label Mulong, Victor has published music tracks for his children's books such as 'Cool Burning', 'The Trees' and 'The Animals'.